Speed Distance Time and Numerical Tests

Useful for the Numerical Part of AOSB Tests

By Vali Nasser

Copyright © 2014

E-book editions may also be available for this title. For more information email: valinasser@gmail.com

All rights reserved by the author. No part of this publication can be reproduced, stored in a retrieval system, or transmitted in any form or by any means, electronic, mechanical, photocopying, recording or otherwise, without the prior permission of the publisher and/or author.

ISBN-13: 978-1495285981

ISBN-10: 1495285987

Jan 2014

Every effort has been made by the author to ensure that the material in this book is up to date and in line with the requirements to pass various types of speed distance time and numerical reasoning tests at the time of publication. The author will also do his best to review, revise and update this material periodically as necessary. However, neither the author nor the publisher can accept responsibility for loss or damage resulting from the material in this book.

Table of Contents

INTRODUCTION 6

CHAPTER 1:   ARITHMETIC PART I 8

Addition and Subtraction using Speed Methods 8

Subtraction 9

Speed Method of Subtraction 10

Subtracting from 100, 1000, 10000, 100000 12

Subtracting from 2000, 3000, 4000, 5000, or more thousands 13

Multiplying & Dividing by 10, 100 and 1000 (by powers of 10) 14

CHAPTER 2:   SPEED DISTANCE AND TIME 18

Some basics first 18

Converting time from 12 hour clock to 24 hour clock see examples below 22

CHAPTER 3: MULTIPLICATION AND DIVISION METHODS THAT MAY BE HELPFUL 23

More methods that may be helpful 24

Division 29

Rounding numbers and estimating 31

CHAPTER 4: ARITHMETIC PART 2 35

Fractions, decimals and percentages 35

Questions involving percentages and fractions 37

2

CHAPTER 5: ARITHMETIC PART 3 FRACTIONS 41

Simplifying fractions 41

Finding fraction of an amount 42

Adding and Subtracting Fractions 43

Adding and subtracting mixed numbers 45

Multiplying Fractions 46

Division of Fractions 46

Multiplying mixed numbers together 48

Dividing mixed numbers together 49

CHAPTER 6: PROPORTIONS AND RATIOS 50

Conversions 53

CHAPTER 7: WEIGHTED AVERAGES & FORMULAE 56

Formula 57

CHAPTER 8: SPEED DISTANCE TIME PRACTICE TESTS 59

Practice Test1 59

Practice Test 2 61

Practice Test 3 63

Practice Test 4 65

Practice Test 5 67

Answers to practice Test 1 69

Answers to practice Test 2..72

Answers to practice Test 3..75

Answers to practice Test 4..78

Answers to practice Test 5..81

Time – Distance graphs...84

CHAPTER 9: NUMBER SEQUENCES 86

CHAPTER 10: PERIMETERS AND VOLUMES OF COMMON SHAPES 89

CHAPTER 11: DATA INTERPRETATION... 93

Mean, Median, Mode and Range 93

Pie Charts 96

Bar charts 99

Line graph..104

CHAPTER 12: BASIC ALGEBRA 107

Multiplying positive and negative numbers...108

Dividing positive and negative numbers...108

Simplifying algebraic expressions 109

Algebraic Substitution 112

Simple Equations..114

PRACTICE TEST 119

ANSWERS TO PRACTICE TEST 122

NUMERICAL REASONING MOCK TEST 125

Mostly Data interpretation with Multiple Choice questions 125

ANSWERS TO MOCK TEST 134

Introduction

This book is aimed at helping you pass the Speed Distance Time and the Numerical Reasoning tests that you can expect during the Army Officer Selection process. Although you will be given other mental aptitude tests too, for example verbal reasoning and abstract reasoning tests, this book **concentrates purely on Speed Distance Time** and **Numerical Reasoning questions**. The numerical reasoning tests are usually multiple choice questions where you need to pick one correct option from the five choices provided. No calculators are provided but you can use paper and pencil. The Speed Distance Time tests are also given to some candidates that are typically given orally. Again no calculators are allowed. The **critical factors** in passing these tests are **accuracy as well as speed**.

Although a lot of the material in the first two chapters will be familiar to you, hopefully you will find some of the **'Speed Methods'** introduced helpful for working out basic questions in arithmetic quickly and will help you to work **within the tight time frames required**. Subsequent chapters will give you examples of how to work out percentages, fractions, proportions, ratios, areas, volumes, speed time and distance questions as well as data interpretation questions. Further, there are practice tests given to help you feel more confident at the test itself.

One thing to remember is that there is often more than one way of working out a given problem. It does not matter which method you use, so long as you feel comfortable with it. You will be marked only for the correct answer. The arithmetic part of the book gives you a variety of methods to choose from, including 'Speed Methods' of calculations.

Finally, although some of you may find the first two chapters very easy and be tempted to skip them, my advice is to go through them quickly to make sure you remind yourself of speed methods of adding and subtracting as well as those of multiplying and dividing without a calculator. **Remember in the actual test you will be working against limited time**. Good luck with your tests.

About the Author

The author of this book has experience in consultancy work and teaching.

The author's initial book 'Speed Mathematics Using the Vedic System' has a significant following and has been translated into Japanese and Chinese as well as German. In addition, his book 'Pass the QTS Numeracy Test with Ease' is very popular with teacher trainees.

Besides being a specialist mathematics teacher the author also has a degree in psychology. This has enabled him to work as an organizational development consultant giving him exposure to psychometric testing particularly applicable to numerical reasoning. Besides working in consultancy he also managed the QTS numeracy tests for teacher trainees at OCR in conjunction with the teaching agency. Subsequently he has tutored and taught mathematics and statistics in schools as well as in adult education.

Chapter 1: Arithmetic part I

Addition and Subtraction using Speed Methods

The normal approach of column addition and subtraction is a good method and if you feel happy with it then you should have no problems with this part of arithmetic. Make sure that when dealing with adding and subtracting decimal numbers, the decimal points are aligned.

The following additional methods will prove useful in increasing your speed which could be a critical part of many numerical reasoning tests

Consider the *Speed Method* below for addition

<u>Compensating or adjusting method</u>

In this method we simply adjust by adding or subtracting from the rounded up or rounded down number as shown in the examples below. In example 1 we round up 96 to 100 and adjust by taking away 4. Similarly we round up 69 to 70 and adjust by taking away 1. See below for all the working out.

Example 1:

96 + 69 =

100 − 4 + 70 − 1 = 170 − 5 = 165

Example 2:

Work out: £1.96 + £3.89

This can be re-written as £2 − 4p + £4 - 11p

= £6 - 15p = £5.85

Example 3:

Work out: 1 hours 52 minutes + 59 minutes

This can be re-written as:

2 hours − 8 minutes + 1 hour − 1 minutes

= 3 hours − 9 minutes = 2 hours 51 minutes

Basic Arithmetic Question

A customer buys three items from a shoe shop, items A, B and C. The selling prices are as follows: A sells for £23.90, B sells for £33.75 and C sells for £19.95. A customer buys all three items. Find the total amount the customer has to pay.

Method:

Total cost = £23.90 + £33.75 + £19.95

= £24 - 10p + £34 - 25p + £20 − 5p = £24 + £34 + £20 - 10p - 25p - 5p

= £78 − 40p = £77.60

Subtraction

You probably remember column subtraction and the number line method from your GCSE days or from when you last did maths. Before we go on to use the *'Speed Method'* let us revisit the familiar method for subtraction.

Example1:

Work out: 241 - 28

Traditional column method

The traditional methods of subtraction serve us well in mathematics. However, there is one more strategy that we can use to make this process much easier but more of this later. First we will consider the normal approach.

Consider the following example:

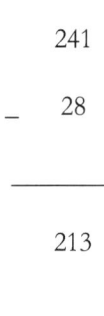

$$241$$
$$-\ \ 28$$
$$\overline{}$$
$$213$$
$$\overline{}$$

Starting from the right hand side we cannot subtract 8 from 1 so we borrow 1 from the tens column to make the units column 11. Subtracting 8 from 11 gives us 3, however since we have taken away 1 from the tens column we are left with 3 in this column. Subtracting 2 from 3 in the tens column gives us 1. Since we have nothing else to take away the final answer is 213.

Speed Method of Subtraction

Example1: Now consider the same problem using a *Speed Method*.

If we add 2 to the top and bottom number we get:

$$243 \quad (241+2)$$
$$-\ \ 30 \quad (28+2)$$
$$\overline{}$$
$$\underline{\ \ \ \ 213}$$

You can see that subtracting 30 from 243 is easier than subtracting 28 from 241!

This strategy relies on the algebraic fact that if you add or subtract the same number from the top and bottom numbers you do not change the answer to the subtraction sum.

So essentially we try and add or subtract a certain number to both the numbers in order to make the sum simpler. A few more examples will help.

Example 2:

$$113$$
$$-\ 6$$

Add 4 to both numbers (we want to try to make the units column 0 in the bottom row if we can and if it helps) So the new sum is:

$$117$$
$$-\ 10$$
$$107$$

We can see that if we subtract 10 from 117 we get 107.

Example 3:

$$321$$
$$-\ 114$$

Let us add 6 to each number so that the unit column in the bottom number becomes a 0 as shown below:

327 (add 6 to 321)

- 120 (add 6 to 114)

207

Subtracting 120 from 327 we get 207 as shown. No borrowing is required.

Note: Sometimes you might find the method above useful; at other times it is easier to revert to the traditional method.

Subtracting from 100, 1000, 10000, 100000

Some people find subtracting from 1000, 10000 or 100000 difficult, so let us consider a useful technique for doing this.

Subtracting from 100, 1000 or 10000 using a '*Speed Method*'

In this case we use the rule **'all from nine and the last from 10'**

Example 1: 100 -76

We simply take each figure (except the last) in 76 from 9 and the last from 10 as shown below:

$$\begin{array}{r} 100 \\ -76 \\ \hline 24 \end{array}$$

Take 7 from 9 to give 2 and take 6 from 10 to give 4

Example 2: 1000 – 897 =103

We simply take each figure (except the last) in 897 from 9 and the last from 10 as shown below:

$$\begin{array}{r} 1000 \\ -897 \\ \hline 103 \end{array}$$

(Take 8 from 9 to give 1. Take 9 from 9 to give 0 and take 7 from 10 to give 3)

Subtracting from 2000, 3000, 4000, 5000, or more thousands

From the above, use the principle of 'last from 10 and the rest from nine' and 'subtracting 1 from the first digit on the left after all the zeros'

Example 1: Work out 3000 – 347

Using the principle of 'last from 10 the rest from nine' and 'subtracting 1 from the first digit on the left after all the zeros'.

We get the answer to be 2653

Example 2: Work out 7000 – 462

Similarly, the answer in this case is 6538.

Typical Question

At a pharmaceutical company a scientist has 10000 Milliliters of a particular liquid which she uses for her experiments. She uses up 8743 Milliliters after several experimental tests. How much does she have left?

Method:

$$\begin{array}{r} 10000 \\ -8743 \\ \hline 1257 \end{array}$$

(Take 8 from 9 to give 1, 7 from 9 to give 2, 4 from 9 to give 5 and finally 3 from 10 to give 7)

This means the scientist has 1257 milliliters of liquid left.

Multiplying & Dividing by 10, 100 and 1000 (by powers of 10)

You are expected to be familiar with multiplying and dividing numbers by 10, 100, 1000 or any other power of 10

Speed Method: Rule for multiplying whole numbers:

(1) When multiplying a whole number by 10 add a zero at the end of the number.

(2) When multiplying by 100 add two zeros.

(3) When multiplying by 1000 add three zeros

(4) You simply add the number of zeros reflected in the power of 10.

Some examples will illustrate this:

(1) 45 X 10 = 450 (add 1 zero to 45)
(2) 67 X 100 = 6700 (add 2 zeros to 67)
(3) 65 X 1000 = 65000 (add 3 zeros to 65)
(4) 65788 X 1000000 = 65788000000 (add 6 zeros to 65788)

Speed Method: Rules for numbers with decimals:

When multiplying by 10, 100, 1000 move the decimal place the appropriate number of places to the right.

(1) 67.5 X 10 = 675 (the decimal point is moved 1 place to the right to give us 675.0 which is the same as 675)

(2) 67.5 X 100 = 6750 (this time move the decimal point two places to the right to give 6750.0 which is the same as 6750)

(3) 6.87 X 1000 = 6870 (in this case move the decimal point three places to the right to give the required answer.)

Now consider examples involving division by 10, 100 and 1000 and other powers of ten.

(1) 450 ÷ 10 = 45 (You simply remove one zero from the number)

(2) 5600 ÷ 100 = 56 (This time you remove two zeros from the number)

(3) 45 ÷ 100 = 0.45 (No zeros to remove – so this time move the decimal point two places to the left to give us 0.45)

(4) 345.78 ÷ 100 = 3.4578 (Again simply move the decimal point 2 places to the left to give the answer)

(5) 456.78 ÷ 1000 = 0.45678 (Move the decimal point 3 places to the left as shown)

(6) 458 ÷ 0.1 = 4580 (remember 0.1 means one–tenth, so dividing a number by 0.1 or one-tenth means the answer becomes 10 times bigger.)

Questions involving powers of 10

(1) Divide 27000 Milliliters by 100

(2) What is 78.87 multiplied by 1000?

(3) What is 67 divided by 100?

(4) What is 687 divided by 0.1? (Tip: Dividing by 0.1 is the same as dividing by one tenth, the answer should thus be 10× bigger))

Using the methods shown earlier the answers are:

(1) 270 ml (2) 78870 (3) 0.67 (4) 6870

If you feel comfortable with the methods above you can skip the traditional method below - although if you have time it will add to your conceptual understanding and will help explain why the 'speed method' leads to the correct answers. If you decide to skip the next bit make sure you look at the last part to do with large and small numbers.

Traditional method of multiplying by 10

The traditional method of multiplying by a 10, 100, 1000 is shown below. This method is useful as it cements the conceptual understanding required. Consider having to work out 34 × 10

Consider place value. For example for the number 34, the right hand digit is the units digit and the number 3 on the left hand side is the tens digit or column. In fact every time you move one place to the left you increase the value by 10. So moving left by one place from the tens column we get the 100's column as shown below.

Hundreds	Tens	Units
	3	4

When we multiply by 10 each digit moves one column to the left. So 34 × 10 = 340 as shown below. In other words 3 tens becomes 3 hundreds, the 4 units becomes 4 tens as shown. Also notice we have 0 units so we must put a zero in the units column. Moving each digit 1 place to the left has the effect of making it 10 × bigger.

Hundreds	Tens	Units
3	4	0

Consider the sum 34 × 100

Multiplying by 100 is similar. We simply multiply by 10 and then 10 again. This has the effect of moving each digit two places to the left. This makes it 100 × bigger.

The number 34 is shown below as 3 tens and 4 units.

Thousands	Hundreds	Tens	Units
		3	4

We will now do the multiplication and see its effect.

Clearly multiplying 34 by 100 has the effect of moving the 3 in the tens column to the thousands column and the 4 units to the hundreds column. This is shown below.

Thousands	Hundreds	Tens	Units
3	4	0	0

So 34 × 100 = 3400 as shown above.

This technique is important as it illustrates the concept of multiplying by 10 or 100 taking place. The same process applies to multiplying by 1000, 10,000 or a higher power of 10.

Also note, there is a short hand way of writing 100, 1000, 10,000 and larger powers of 10.

$100 = 10^2$ (10 squared, which is 10 X 10)

$1000 = 10^3$ (10 cubed which is 10 X 10 X 10)

$10,000 = 10^4$ ((10 to the power 4, which is 10 X 10 X 10 X 10)

$1000,000 = 10^6$ (10 to the power 6 which is 10 X 10 X 10 X 10 X 10 X 10)

Higher powers can be written similarly.

Dividing by 10, 100 and 1000

Conceptually, dividing by 10, 100 or 1000 is a similar process, except, on this occasion, you move the digits to the right by the appropriate number of places.

Consider having to divide 34 by 10.

Here 3 tens and 4 units becomes 3 units and 4 tenths as shown.

Hundreds	Tens	Units	Tenths
		3	4

The rationale for this is that we move each digit to the right. So 3 tens becomes 3 units and 4 units becomes 4 tenths as shown above. The answer is written as 3.4. Similarly, when dividing by 100 or a 1000 the number is moved two and three places to the right as appropriate. We will now look at the technique below to work out the answer mechanically. This ensures you get the right answer without having to resort to the thousands, hundreds, tens, units, tenths and hundredths column. The simple rules shown below may help those students who find the above process difficult.

Chapter 2: Speed Distance and Time

Some basics first

You already know that 1 hour = 60 minutes and $\frac{1}{2}$ hour = 30 minutes or 0.5 hours.

Also note that:

$\frac{1}{4}$ hour = 15 minutes or 0.25 hours

2.5 hours = $2\frac{1}{2}$ hours or 2 hours 30minutes (0.5 hours = half of 60 minutes)

2.25 hours = $2\frac{1}{4}$ hours or 2hrs 15 minutes

Further points to note:

2.4 hours = 2 hours 24 minutes (0.4 hours = 0.4X60 = 24 minutes)

2.1 hours = 2 hours 6 minutes (0.1hours = 0.1 X 60 = 6 minutes)

(For other time based questions e.g. years, months, days, hours, minutes or seconds remember the appropriate units)

Example 1: Peter completes a lap in 2.3 minutes. How many minutes and seconds is this?

Method: Convert 0.3 minutes into seconds. Since one whole minute = 60 seconds, then 0.3 minutes = 0.3X60 = 18 seconds. Hence Peter completes the lap in 2 minutes and 18 seconds.

(Note that 0.3 X 60 is the same as 3 X 6, hence this is equivalent to 18)

Example 2: What is $\frac{3}{4}$ hours in minutes?

Method: We know that $\frac{1}{2}$ hour is 30 minutes and $\frac{1}{4}$ hour is 15 minutes. Hence $\frac{3}{4}$ hours = $(\frac{1}{2}+\frac{1}{4})$ = 30 minutes + 15 minutes = **45 minutes**

Example 3: Convert 40 minutes into a fraction of an hour.

Method: We know there are 60 minutes in an hour. So 40 minutes represents $\frac{40}{60}$ of an hour which simplifies to $\frac{4}{6} = \frac{2}{3}$ hour (divide top and bottom of $\frac{4}{6}$ by 2 to get $\frac{2}{3}$)

Tip: <u>Memorize these basic time conversions</u>

60 minutes = 1 hour

45 minutes = $\frac{3}{4}$ hour

30 minutes = $\frac{1}{2}$ hour

15 minutes = $\frac{1}{4}$ hour

20 minutes = $\frac{1}{3}$ hour

10 minutes = $\frac{1}{6}$ hour

5 minutes = $\frac{1}{12}$ hour

1 minute = $\frac{1}{60}$ hour

Now let us look at some typical questions involving Speed, Distance and Time. Firstly try and remember the following formulas.

$\text{Speed} = \frac{Distance}{Time}$ or *Distance ÷ Time*

Distance = *Speed × Time*

$\text{Time} = \frac{Distance}{Speed}$ or *Distance ÷ Speed*

Example 1:

What is the distance travelled if my speed is 60kmh and I travel for 1 hour and 30 minutes?

As you can see from above the formula for working out the distance depends on the speed and time taken in the appropriate units.

D = S×T where D is the distance, S the speed and T is the time.

1 hour 30 minutes corresponds to 1.5 hours so, using the formula, **D = 60×1.5 = 90 km**. That is, the distance equals 90km

Example 2:

Work out the average speed at which I travel if I cover 100 miles in 2.5 hours.

The formula for working out the speed is given as **Speed= Distance/Time**

That is **S = D÷T**

Since S = D÷T, **this means S = 100÷2.5 =40 mph** (Notice the units for the first example were in **kilometres and units for the second example were in miles**)

Example 3:

Calculate the time taken to cover 90 miles if I travel at 60mph?

The formula for working out time taken is given by **T = D÷S**

so T = 90÷60 = 9÷6 =3÷ 2 = **1.5 hours** or 1 hour and 30 minutes.

Earlier we saw the formula: **S = D ÷T**, that is, Speed $= \dfrac{\text{Distance}}{\text{Time}}$.

Another method of remembering these formulas is by drawing a triangle as shown below and covering up the parameter or the variable that you want to find.

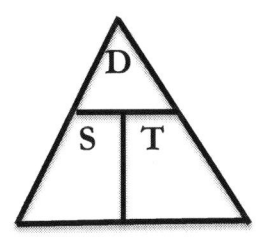

```
      /D\
     /___\
    / S|T \
   /___|___\
```

So for example D = S × T

Method: Cover up the variable you want to find, in this case D (distance) so we get **D = S × T**

Similarly, $S = \frac{D}{T}$ and $T = \frac{D}{S}$

Intuitive method if you forget the formulas

Make up a simple problem yourself and see how to work out the relevant questions as shown below.

Example1: If I travel at 30mph **then I travel 30 miles in 1 hour, in 2 hours I travel 60 miles, in 3 hours I travel 90 miles** and so on. **So Distance = Speed × Time**

Example 2: If I travel 100 miles in 1 hour, then I travel 200 miles in 2 hours, 300 miles in 3 hours so my speed must be 100 miles per hour. **So Speed = Distance ÷ Time**

Example3: If I travel at 100 mph and cover 100 miles then clearly it will take me twice as long (2 hours) to cover 200 miles and 3 times as long (3 hours) to cover 300 miles. **So Time = $\frac{Distance}{speed}$**

Converting time from 12 hour clock to 24 hour clock see examples below

12 –Hour Clock	24 –Hour Clock
8.45 am	08:45
11.30 am	11:30
12.20pm	12:20
2.35 pm	14: 35 (after 12pm add the appropriate minutes and hours to 12 hours, in this case 2hrs 35mins +12hrs = 14:35)
8.45 pm	20:45 (8hrs 45mins + 12hrs = 20:45)
11.47pm	23:47 (11hrs 47mins +12hrs = 23:47)

The Convention is that if the time is in 24-hr clock there is no need to put hrs after the time.

Chapter 3: Multiplication and Division methods that may be helpful

Example 1: At a company new candidates are mentored once a week for 12 minutes each. There are 15 candidates who are being mentored. There is also a break for 20 minutes. The session starts at 11.30am. When does it finish? Give your answer using the 24 hour clock

Method: Clearly we need to first work out the total time it takes for all the candidates. Total time for 15 candidates is 15 X 12 = (15 X10 +15x2) =180 minutes = 3 hours plus break time of 20 minutes. So the mentoring session ends 3hrs and 20 minutes after 11.30am – this means it ends at 2.50pm. However using the 24 hour clock the times it ends is 14:50

Example 2: Peter completes a lap in 2.3 minutes. How many minutes and seconds is this?

Method: Convert 0.3 minutes into seconds. Since one whole minute = 60 seconds, then 0.3 minutes = 0.3X60 = 18 seconds. Hence Peter completes the lap in 2 minutes and 18 seconds.

(Note that 0.3 X 60 is the same as 3 X 6, hence this is equivalent to 18)

General Multiplication questions

Example1 There are 4 medium size boxes containing 18 black jumpers each and 3 bigger boxes containing 23 black jumpers each. How many black jumpers are there altogether?

Method: 4 boxes of 18 each imply there are 4 × 18 = 72 black jumpers

(Another way of working out 4 × 18 is to break it down as follows: 4 × 18 = 4 × 10 + 4 ×8 = 40 + 32 =72)

Similarly, 3 boxes of 23 each means, 3 × 23 =69 black jumpers

Finally, 72 + 69 = 70 +2 + 60 + 9 = 130 + 11 =141

There are a total of 141 black jumpers altogether

Example2

I buy 5 books for £3.97 each. How much change do I get from a £20 note?

Method: Round up each book to £4. Hence the cost of 5 books = £4×5 – 5×3p = £20 - 15p = £19. 85

You can see straight away that I get 15p change from my £20 note

More methods that may be helpful

The Grid Method of Multiplication

This is a very powerful method for those who find traditional long multiplication methods difficult.

Example1: Multiply 37 × 6

Re-write the number 37 as 30 and 7 and re-write as shown in the grid table.

×	30	7
6	180	42

Now simply add up all the numbers inside the grid. So the answer is 180+42 =222

Example 2: work out 15 × 13

To work this out using the grid method, re-write 15 as 10 and 5, and 13 as 10 and 3 as shown on the outside of the grid table.

×	10	5
10	100	50
3	30	15

Multiply out the outside horizontal numbers with the outside vertical numbers to get the numbers inside as shown. Finally, just add up the inside numbers which in this case is 100+50+30+15 =195

Multiplication with decimals

Example3: Work out 1.5 × 1.3

Step1: Leave out the decimal points and just work out the answer to 15 × 13 as shown above.

We know the answer to this is 195.

Step2: Now count the number of digits there are from the right before the decimal place for each number being multiplied and add them up. That is one for the first number and one for the second number to give a total of 2.

Step3: In the answer 195 count two from the right hand side and insert the decimal point.

So the answer is 1.95

Example 4: Work out 0.15 × 1.3

We know the answer to 15 × 13 is 195

This time the number of digits for each number before the decimal point is 2 for the first number and 1 for the second number giving a total of 3.

25

We now count 3 places from the right and insert a decimal point.

So the answer is 0.195

If you want to you can think of getting the answer another way:

Consider **Example 3** again: Multiply 1.5 × 1.3

We know the answer is 195. Note the fact that 1.5 is 15 divided by 10 and 1.3 is 13 divided by 10. So the answer is simply 195 divided by 10×10 =100, so we divide 195 by 100 to get the answer as 1.95

More Multiplication

We will look at some fascinating ways of quickly multiplying by 11, 9, and 5, which will help you speed up your number work in mental arithmetic

Multiplying quickly by 11

One common method used is to multiply by 10 and then add the number itself. We will now look at a super- efficient method that is rarely used.

Super-efficient Speed Method:

11 × 11 =121 (the first and last digits remain the same & the middle number is the sum of the first two digits)

The basic method is: Start with the first digit, add the next two, until the last one. This method works with any number of digits.

Let us explore a few more examples with two digit numbers.

13 × 11= 143 (Keep the first and last digit of the number 13 the same, add 1 & 3 to give the middle number 4)

14 × 11= 154

19 × 11= 1(10)9=209 (Notice the middle number is 10, since 1+9=10, so we need to carry 1 to the left hand number)

A few more examples will show the power of this method.

27 × 11= 297 (the first number=2, the middle number=2+7, the last number =7)

28 × 11=2(10)8= 308 (using similar analysis to 19 X 11 above)

The same principle applies to numbers with more than 2 digits.

Example: Work out 215 × 11

Method: Keep the first and the last digit the same. Starting from the first digit add the subsequent digit to get the next digit, do this again with the second digit until the last digit which stays the same. So, 215 × 11 =2365 (2, is the first digit so stays the same, the sum of 2 and 1 gives you the next digit 3, the sum of 1 and 5 gives you the third digit 6 and finally the last digit 5 stays the same)

Example involving multiplying by 11

In a certain company 54 insurance agents manage to sell 11 insurance policies each in a particular month.

How many insurance policies did these agents sell altogether in that month?

54 × 11 using the method explained above is 594

Hence, total insurance policies sold in this month by these agents = 594 (Method: Keep the first and last digit of the number 54 he same, add 5 & 4 to give the middle number 9)

Multiplying quickly by 9

Here is an easy method to work out the 9× table

Example 1: Work out 9×7

Method

Step1: Add '0' to the number you are going to multiply by 9, e.g. 7 to get 70

Step2: Now subtract 7 from 70 to get 63 which is the final answer

Example 2: Work out 9 × 35

Method

Step1: Add '0' to the number you are going to multiply by 9, i.e. 35 to get 350

Step2: Now subtract 35 from 350 to get 315 which is the final answer

Example 3: Work out 9 × 78

Method

Step1: Add '0' to the number you are going to multiply by 9, e.g. 78 to get 780

Step2: Now subtract 78 from 780 to get 702 which is the final answer

A quick way of multiplying by 5

Multiply the number by 10 and halve the answer.

Example 1: 5 × 4 = half of 10 × 4 = half of 40 = 20

Example 2: 5 × 16 = half of 10 × 16 = half of 160 = 80

Example 3: 5 × 23 = half of 10 × 23 = half of 230 = 115

TIP: Remember the Order of Arithmetical Operations

Remembering the order in which you do arithmetical operations is very important.

The rule taught traditionally is that of **BIDMAS**.

The **BIDMAS** rule is as follows:

(1) Always work out the **B**racket(s) first
(2) Then work out the **I**ndices of a number (squares, cubes, square roots and so on)
(3) Now **M**ultiply and **D**ivide
(4) Finally do the **A**ddition and **S**ubtraction.

Example 1: Work out 2 + 8×3

Do the multiplication before the addition

So 8×3 =24 then add 2 to get 26

Example 2: 4 + 13(7 – 2) this means add 4 to 13× (7 – 2)

Do the **brackets first** so 7 – 2 =5, **then multiply** 5 by 13 to get 65 and **finally add** 4 to get 69

Summary: When working out sums involving mixed operations (e.g. +, - , x and ÷) you need to work out the steps in stages using the BIDMAS rule: So to work out 8 +25 ×12

Do the multiplication first, 25×12 =300, write down 300 then add 8 to get the answer 308.

Division

In general the traditional short division approach is a good method. However, there are some other smart techniques worth considering for special situations.

Dividing a number by 2 is a very useful skill, since if you can divide by 2, you can by halving it again divide by 4 and halving it again divide by 8.

Dividing by 2, 4 and 8

Simply halve the number to divide by 2

(Some find it difficult to halve a number like 13. An alternative strategy is to multiply the number by 5 and divide by 10)

Halving again is the same as dividing by 4

And halving once more is the same as dividing by 8

Example 1: 28 ÷ 2 =14

Example 2: 268 ÷ 4 =134 ÷ 2 = 67

Example 3: 568 ÷ 8 = 284 ÷ 4 = 142 ÷ 2 = 71

Example 4: 65 ÷ 4 = 32.5 ÷ 2 = 16.25

Dividing by 5

An easy way to do this is to multiply the number by 2 and divide by 10.

Example 1: 120 ÷ 5 = (120 X 2) ÷ 10 = 240 ÷ 10 = 24

Example 2: 127 ÷ 5 = (127 X 2) ÷ 10 = 254 ÷ 10 = 25.4

Similarly to divide by 50 simply multiply by 2 and divide by 100

Dividing by 25

A good way to do this is to multiply by 4 and divide by 100.

Example1: 240 ÷ 25 = (240 X 4) ÷ 100 = 960 ÷ 100 = 9.6

Example2: 700 ÷ 25 = (700 X 4) ÷ 100 = 2800 ÷ 100 = 28

Dividing by other numbers: The conventional short division method is a good method but you might find the speed methods below useful sometimes.

Question involving division: Example1: In one particular week, in a restaurant a bonus of £67.50 is divided amongst three waiters. How much does each one get in that week?

Clearly this is the same as 60 ÷ 3 added to 7.5 ÷ 3

60 ÷ 3 = 20 and 7.5 ÷ 3 = 2.5 which altogether is 22.5

Hence, £67.5 ÷ 3 = £22.50 per waiter

Example 1: Divide 145 by 7

(145 = 140 + 5)

We can say that 140 ÷ 7 = 20, and then we are left with 5/7. So the answer is 20 and 5/7

Example 2: Divide 103 ÷ 9

(103 = 99 + 4) = 99 ÷ 9 + 4/9 = 11 and 4/9

Square numbers and square roots

You probably remember that squaring a number is simply multiplying a number by itself. So 4^2 means $4 \times 4 = 16$, 12^2 means $12 \times 12 = 144$ and so on.

The square root is written like this $\sqrt{}$ and means finding a number which when multiplied by itself gives you the number inside the square root.

Example 1: Find $\sqrt{16}$. The answer is clearly 4. Since $4 \times 4 = 16$

Let us consider some other square roots.

(1) $\sqrt{81}$, (2) $\sqrt{144}$, (3) $\sqrt{64}$, (4) $\sqrt{169}$, (5) $\sqrt{196}$, (6) $\sqrt{225}$, (7) $\sqrt{256}$, (8) $\sqrt{324}$, (9) $\sqrt{400}$

Answers: (1) = 9, (2) = 12, (3) = 8, (4) = 13, (5) = 14, (6) = 15 and (7) = 16, (8) = 18 and (9) = 20

Rounding numbers and estimating

We will start simply with rounding numbers to the nearest 10 and 100

Consider the number 271

Rounded to the nearest 10 this number is 270

Rounded to the nearest 100 this number is 300

(The principle is that if the right hand digit is lower than 5 you drop this number and replace it by 0. Conversely if the number is 5 or more drop that digit and add 1 to the left)

Try a few more:

5382 to the nearest 10 is 5380

5382 to the nearest hundred is 5400

5382 to the nearest 1000 is 5000

This rule can also be applied to decimal numbers:

3.7653 rounded to the nearest thousandth is 3.765

3.7653 rounded to the nearest hundredth is 3.77

3.7653 rounded to the nearest tenth is 3.8

3.7653 rounded to the nearest unit is 4

Tip: remember to use common sense when rounding in real life situations:

Example: A book store wants to keep 120 books in the same size boxes. They can fit 22 books in a box. How many boxes will they need?

Method: Number of boxes required will be 120÷22= 5.5 (to one decimal place). But clearly, they cannot have 5.5 boxes. So they need to have 6 boxes

Estimating calculations quickly

Example 1: I travel 39.5 miles in 1 hour and 58 minutes. What is my **approximate** speed?

39.5 miles is approximately 40 miles. Also 1 hour 58 minutes is approximately 2 hours. We know that Speed = Distance ÷ Time. This means my speed is **approximately** 40 ÷ 2 = 20 mph

Example 2: Work out 38 × 2.9 × 0.53

We can approximate 38 to be 40 to the nearest ten, we can approximate 2.9 o 3 to the nearest unit. We can approximate 0.53 to 0.5 to the nearest tenth. So the magnitude of the answer is 40 × 3 × 0.5. This is 120 × 0.5 =60 (approximately)

Example 3: I travel 398.5 miles from A to B and 495.3 miles from B to C. **Estimate** the total mileage I cover from A to B to C.

Clearly, 398.5 miles is approximately 400 miles and 495.3 miles is approximately 500 miles. So my total estimated distance covered from A to B to C is 400 + 500 = 900 miles approximately.

More Number Work: (basic reminders):

Integers: These are whole numbers that include both positive and negative numbers including 0. So for example ....-5,-4,-3,-2, 0, 1, 2, 3, 4, ...are all integers.

Even Numbers: All numbers that have 2 as a factor are even numbers.

Examples are: 2, 4, 6, 8, 10, 12, 14, 16

So, 168 is an even number as it can be divided exactly by 2.

Odd Numbers: Are all numbers that do not have 2 as a factor.

Examples: 1, 3, 5, 7, 9, 11, 13, 15, 17

So for example 81 is an odd number, as 2 is not a factor of 81.

Notice something interesting about odd numbers. The cumulative sum of consecutive odd numbers generates square numbers.

The first number is $1 = 1 \times 1 = 1^2$

The sum of the first two numbers is $1 + 3 = 4 = 2 \times 2 = 2^2$

The sum of the first three numbers is $1 + 3 + 5 = 9 = 3 \times 3 = 3^2$

The sum of the first four numbers is $1 + 3 + 5 + 7 = 16 = 4 \times 4 = 4^2$ and so on.

Multiples: These are simply numbers in the multiplication tables.

For example the multiples of 6 are 6, 12, 18, 24, 30, …..

Factors: A factor is a number that divides exactly into another number as for example, the number 2 in the case of even numbers.

3 is a factor of 9, as 3 goes exactly into 9.

15, has two factors other than 15 and 1. The two factors are 5 and 3, since both these numbers go exactly into 15. **Example:** Find all the factors of 21. The factors are: 1, 3, 7 and 21 (since all these numbers divide exactly into 21)

Prime numbers: A prime number is a natural number that can be divided only by itself and by 1 (without a remainder). For example, 11 can be divided only by 1 and by 11. Prime numbers are whole numbers greater than 1. So for example the first 10 prime numbers are: 2, 3, 5, 7, 11, 13, 17, 19, 23 and 29. **Be careful that an odd number is not necessarily a prime number.** For example 9 is not a prime number as its factors are 1, 3 and 9 and **prime numbers should have only two factors, 1 and the number itself. Also, note that 2 is a prime number, the only even number that can be divided by 1 and itself!**

Chapter 4: Arithmetic Part 2

Fractions, decimals and percentages

I am sure most of you are aware that $\frac{1}{2}=0.5$. This in turn is equal to 50%.

It is worth reviewing this fact. In addition, you should try and remember the following other equivalences if you have forgotten them:

Fractions, decimals and percentage equivalents

Fractions	Decimal	Percentage
$\frac{1}{2}$	0.5	50%
$\frac{1}{4}$	0.25	25%
$\frac{3}{4}$	0.75	75%
$\frac{1}{10}$	0.1	10%
$\frac{1}{5}$	0.2	20%

If, we know $\frac{1}{2} = 0.5$

We can deduce that $\frac{1}{4} = 0.25$

(Since a quarter is half of half)

Similarly $\frac{1}{8}$ is **0.125**

We can do this quickly because all we do is halve each decimal value.

Half of 0.5 is 0.25, Half of 0.25 is 0.125

We can of course continue this process.

Further if we know $\frac{1}{10} = 0.1$ we can now work out $\frac{2}{10}, \frac{3}{10}, \frac{7}{10}$ etc.

$\frac{2}{10} = 0.2$ (2 × 0.1), $\frac{3}{10} = 0.3$ (3 × 0.1), $\frac{7}{10} = 0.7$ (7 × 0.1), $\frac{9}{10} = 0.9$ (9 × 0.1)

Another useful fraction and decimal equivalent to remember is $\frac{1}{3} = 0.333...$ (0.3 recurring)

The key equivalent percentages to remember are as follows:

$\frac{3}{4} = 75\%$, $\frac{1}{2} = 50\%$, $\frac{1}{4} = 25\%$, $\frac{1}{8} = 12.5\%$, $\frac{1}{10} = 10\%$

See summary box below

Summary:

Remember the following equivalences

$\frac{1}{2}=0.5=50\%$, $\frac{1}{4}=0.25=25\%$, $\frac{3}{4}=0.75=75\%$, $\frac{1}{10}=0.1=10\%$

Also if you can try to remember, $\frac{1}{5}=0.2=20\%$, and $\frac{2}{5}=0.4=40\%$, $\frac{1}{3}=0.333\ldots$ (0.3 recurring) = 33.33% (to 2 decimal places)

To convert a fraction into a percentage, simply multiply the fraction by 100

Questions involving percentages and fractions

Example 1: Find 25% of £250

Method: Find 50% of £250 and halve it again.

Half of £250 = £125, Half of £125 = £62.50, so 25% of £250 = £62.50

Example 2: In a marketing department of 25 people there are 12 women and the rest are men.

(1) What fraction of the marketing department consists of men?

(2) What percentage is this?

(1) Since there are 12 women, there are 13 men out of 25. So the fraction of men is $\frac{13}{25}$

(2) The percentage of men is $\frac{13}{25} \times 100 = 52\%$, (Divide 100 by 25 to get 4. Then multiply 13 by 4 to get 52%)

Example 3: 30% of the applicants for a certain job are male. There are 30 candidates in total. How many of the applicants are female?

Method: If 30% of the applicants are male, this means 70% are female. So we need to find 70% of 30 candidates. Since 10% of 30 is 3, this means 70% corresponds to 3X7 = 21 females. Hence, 21 of the candidates are female.

Working out increase or decrease in percentages from original value

Example1: In a certain corner shop 16 packs of cereal A were sold in week 1. In the same shop 20 packs of the same cereal were sold in week 2. What was the percentage increase in the cereal packs A sold from week 1 to week 2?

Method: Increase in number of cereal packs A = 20 – 16 = 4. Original number of cereal packs =16. The increase of 4 was based on 16 cereal packs. To work out the percentage increase we simply divide the increase by the original number of cereal packs and multiply this by 100. That is $\frac{4}{16} \times 100 = \frac{1}{4} \times 100 = 25\%$

To work out decrease in percentages (uses the same principle as above)

Example2: The original price of a projector was: £150, the new price is reduced to £135. What is the percentage decrease in price? The decrease in price is £150 - £135 = £15. The decrease over the original price is $\frac{15}{150}$. To turn this into a percentage we multiply $\frac{15}{150} \times 100 = \frac{1500}{150} = 10\%$. So the decrease in percentage price is 10%.

The basic formula to work out increase or decrease percentage change is shown below:

$$\frac{difference\ between\ final\ and\ original\ value}{original\ value} \times 100$$

One thing to remember though is that the increase or decrease in percentage points is different from increase or decrease in percentages.

To illustrate this consider the example below:

The unemployment rate in a region A was 8% in 2010. In 2011 the unemployment rate in the same region was 10%. **(1)** What was the **percentage point** increase in unemployment from 2010 to 2011? **(2)** What is the **percentage increase** in unemployment from 2010 to 2011?

(1) The **percentage point** increase is simply 2% (i.e. from 8% to 10%)

(2) However the **percentage increase** in unemployment is $\frac{2}{8} \times 100 = \frac{200}{8} = \frac{100}{4} = 25\%$.

In the Numerical reasoning test context, if you are asked to work out the **percentage point increase,** say in sales in Product A changing from 20% to 30%. The answer is obviously 10%. But if asked to work out the **percentage increase**, then the answer is $\frac{10}{20} \times 100 = \frac{1000}{20} = \frac{100}{2} = 50\%$

Miscellaneous questions involving fractions and percentages

Example 1: Finding fraction of an amount

Find $\frac{3}{4}$ of £600, First find $\frac{1}{2}$ = £300, then find $\frac{1}{4}$ (which is half of half) = £150

Therefore $\frac{3}{4}$ = £450 (adding half plus a quarter)

Example 2: Finding a fraction and turning it into a percentage

There are 40 builders in a small town in Yorkshire. In a particular month 5 builders are without work.

What is the percentage of builders that do not have work in this month in this small town?

The fraction of builders without work = $\frac{5}{40}$, by dividing top and bottom numbers by 5 we get $\frac{1}{8}$.

To convert 1/8 into a percentage simply multiply 1/8 by 100

= 1/8 x100 =100/8 = 50/4 =25/2 =12.5%

(Another method: We know ¼ =25%

Hence 1/8 =12.5% (Since 1/8 is half of a quarter)

Chapter 5:   Arithmetic Part 3   Fractions

Simplifying fractions

Reducing a fraction to its lowest terms

Basically you need to find numbers that divide into the top number (numerator) as well as the bottom number (denominator), and then divide them both by the same number (start with 2, if doesn't go then choose 3, then 5, and then the next prime factor e.g. 7, 11, etc.)

Example1: Reduce $\frac{16}{24}$ to its lowest terms.

8 divides exactly into 16 and 24, so in the fraction $\frac{16}{24}$ divide top and bottom by 8. This gives the answer as $\frac{2}{3}$

In case you can't see this straight away, try starting with the number two and work your way numerically upwards using the next prime factor i.e. try 3, then 5 etc. if required

So for the fraction $\frac{16}{24}$ we can start dividing top and bottom by 2 to give us $\frac{8}{12}$, then do the same again as both 8 and 12 are still divisible by 2. This gives us $\frac{4}{6}$ and finally repeating the process once more reduces the fraction to $\frac{2}{3}$ which is the simplest form.

Example 2

Simplify $\frac{9}{12}$ to its lowest terms

In this case we can't divide top and bottom by 2, so we try 3. Since 3 will go into both 9 and 12, we can reduce this to the fraction $\frac{3}{4}$ (since 9 ÷ 3 = 3 and 12 ÷ 3 = 4)

Hence, $\frac{9}{12}$ reduces to $\frac{3}{4}$

Example 3:

Reduce fraction $\frac{49}{77}$ to its lowest terms. This time we need to spot that 2, 3, 5, does not go into either 49, or 77. Either by trial and error or by spotting the right number we notice 7 goes into both the numerator and the denominator. This reduces $\frac{49}{77}$ to $\frac{7}{11}$

Cancelling down a fraction to its simplest form (lowest term)

To simplify a fraction to its lowest terms you divide the numerator and the denominator by the same prime factors (2, 3, 5, 7, 11, etc.) to give the equivalent fractions as shown in the examples above

---

Finding fraction of an amount

Example 1: Find $\frac{2}{5}$ of 25, simply replace the 'of' by ×. (times)

So $\frac{2}{5}$ of 25 becomes $\frac{2}{5} \times 25$

To work this out find out 1/5 of 25 and then multiply the answer by 2. So 25 divided by 5, equals 5, then 2 × 5 =10. Hence $\frac{2}{5}$ of 25 =10.

Example:

60 people apply for a certain job vacancy. 12 people are short-listed for an interview. What is the proportion of people that are not short listed for the interview? Give your answer as a decimal.

Total number of people applying for this job = 60, Since 12 people are shortlisted, this means 48 are not shortlisted. Hence the proportion that is not shortlisted = 48/60. If you divide top and bottom by 6, this simplifies to 8/10.

The answer as a decimal is 0.8

Adding and Subtracting Fractions

This next section will help you revise adding, subtracting, multiplying and dividing fractions together

Consider adding and subtracting fractions together.

When the bottom numbers (denominators) are the same, just add the top numbers together keeping the bottom number the same, likewise for subtraction just subtract the top two numbers.

Example 1: $\dfrac{2}{5} + \dfrac{1}{5} = \dfrac{3}{5}$

Example 2: $\dfrac{2}{5} - \dfrac{1}{5} = \dfrac{1}{5}$

When the denominators are different

Example 3: Work out $\dfrac{1}{2} + \dfrac{2}{5}$

When the denominators are different, the traditional method of doing this is to find the lowest common denominator. We have to find a number that both 2 and 5 will go into. This is clearly 10.

We can now re-write the fraction with the same common denominator.

To do this we have to ask how did we get the denominator from 2 to 10 for the first part, and likewise for the second part from 5 to 10. The answer is shown below:

$$\dfrac{1 \times 5}{2 \times 5} + \dfrac{2 \times 2}{5 \times 2} = \dfrac{5}{10} + \dfrac{4}{10} = \dfrac{9}{10}$$

We had to multiply top and bottom by 5 for the first part and top and bottom by 2 for the second part as shown above. We can then add the fraction as we have the same common denominator.

We can however use another very simple strategy that always works. The method is that of crosswise multiplication.

The basic method is to take the fraction sum and do crosswise multiplication as shown by the arrows. In addition, multiply the denominators (bottom numbers) together to get the new denominator.

Example1: $\dfrac{1}{2} + \dfrac{2}{5} = \dfrac{1}{2} \times \dfrac{2}{5} = \dfrac{1 \times 5 + 2 \times 2}{2 \times 5} = \dfrac{5+4}{10} = \dfrac{9}{10}$

We notice that if we cross multiply as shown we get 1 X 5 and 2 X 2 respectively at the top. To get the bottom number we simply multiply the bottom numbers, 2 and 5 together. So the denominator is 2 X 5=10.

Let us try another example:

Example2: Work out $\dfrac{3}{7} + \dfrac{2}{5}$

Using crosswise multiplication and adding rule, as well as multiplying the bottom two numbers we get:

$\dfrac{3}{7} \times \dfrac{2}{5} = \dfrac{3 \times 5 + 7 \times 2}{35} = \dfrac{15+14}{35} = \dfrac{29}{35}$

This is a very elegant method which always works

Example3: Work out $\dfrac{3}{7} - \dfrac{2}{5}$

This is similar to the above except instead of adding we now subtract as shown below.

$\dfrac{3}{7} \times \dfrac{2}{5} = \dfrac{3 \times 5 - 7 \times 2}{35} = \dfrac{15-14}{35} = \dfrac{1}{35}$

Note: In fact you can use this method when adding or subtracting any fraction that you find difficult. Even if you use this method for simple cases, you will still get the right answer but you may have to cancel down to get the lowest terms for the final answer.

For example we know that $\dfrac{1}{4} + \dfrac{1}{2} = \dfrac{3}{4}$

But if we didn't know and used the method shown we would get $\dfrac{1}{4} \diagup\!\!\!\!\diagdown \dfrac{1}{2} =$
$\dfrac{1X2+4X1}{4X2} = \dfrac{2+4}{8} = \dfrac{6}{8} = \dfrac{3}{4}$ (we get this by dividing both the numerator and denominator in $\dfrac{6}{8}$ by 2). So we get the same answer in the end

Question involving fractions

(1) Find $2\dfrac{3}{4}$ of £64

We first work out 2 X 64 = 128, to work out three quarters of 64 we first work out a half and then add it to a quarter of 64.

Half of £64 is £32

A quarter of £64 (is half of £32) is £16

Hence three quarters of £64 = £32 + £16 = £48

So two and three quarters of £64 = £128 + £48 = £176

Adding and subtracting mixed numbers

We first add or subtract the whole numbers and then the fractional parts.

Example 1: $2\dfrac{2}{5} + 4\dfrac{3}{7}$

Adding the whole numbers we get 6. (Simply add 2 and 4)

Now add the fractional parts to get: $\dfrac{14+15}{35} = \dfrac{29}{35}$

So the answer is $6\dfrac{29}{35}$

Example 2: $4\dfrac{3}{7} - 2\dfrac{2}{5}$

Subtract the whole numbers and then the fractional parts, which gives us:

$2\dfrac{15-14}{35} = 2\dfrac{1}{35}$

Multiplying Fractions

Multiplying fractions by the traditional method is quite efficient so we will consider only this approach.

Example 1: $\dfrac{2}{3} \times \dfrac{5}{7} = \dfrac{10}{21}$

In this case we simply multiply the top two numbers to get the new numerator and multiply the bottom two numbers together to get the new denominator, as shown above.

Another example will help consolidate this process:

Example 2: $\dfrac{10}{21} \times \dfrac{5}{7} = \dfrac{50}{147}$

(Multiply 10 × 5 to get 50 for the numerator and 21 × 7 to get 147 for the denominator)

Division of Fractions

When dividing fractions we invert the second fraction and multiply as shown.

Think of an obvious example. If we have to divide ½ by ¼ we intuitively know that the answer is 2. The reason for this is that there are 2 quarters in one half. Let us see how this works in practice.

Example 1: $\dfrac{1}{2} \div \dfrac{1}{4} = \dfrac{1}{2} \times \dfrac{4}{1} = \dfrac{4}{2} = 2$

Step 1: Re-write fraction as a multiplication sum with the second fraction inverted.

Step 2: Work out the fraction as a normal multiplication

Step 3: Simplify if possible. In this case 4 divided by 2 is 2.

Example 2: $\dfrac{6}{11} \div \dfrac{5}{11} = \dfrac{6}{11} \times \dfrac{11}{5} = \dfrac{66}{55} = \dfrac{6}{5} = 1\dfrac{1}{5}$

Step1: Re-write the fraction inverting the second fraction as shown

Step2: Multiply the top part and the bottom part to get $\dfrac{66}{55}$ as shown.

Step 3: Simplify this by dividing top and bottom by 11 to get $\dfrac{6}{5}$. Now this finally simplifies to $1\dfrac{1}{5}$ as shown.

The following steps are required to convert a mixed number into a fraction. Consider the mixed fraction $2\frac{1}{4}$.

Step 1: Multiply the denominator of the fractional part by the whole number and add the numerator. In this case this works out to $2 \times 4 + 1 = 9$. This now becomes the new numerator.

Step 2: The denominator stays the same as before. Now re-write the new fraction as $\frac{9}{4}$. (That is the new numerator ÷ existing denominator)

Let us look at another example. Convert the mixed number, $3\frac{3}{7}$ into a fraction.

Step 1: Multiply denominator of fractional part by whole number and add the numerator. This gives $3 \times 7+3 = 24$ as the new numerator.

Step2: Re-write fraction as new fraction. This is now the new numerator ÷ existing denominator. This gives us $\frac{24}{7}$

Multiplying mixed numbers together

Consider the examples below:

Example: $1\frac{1}{5} \times 1\frac{3}{8}$

The method is simply to convert both mixed numbers into fractions and multiply as shown below:

$$1\frac{1}{5} \times 1\frac{3}{8} = \frac{6}{5} \times \frac{11}{8} = \frac{66}{40} = 1\frac{26}{40} = 1\frac{13}{20}$$

(Notice $\frac{26}{40}$ simplifies to $\frac{13}{20}$)

Dividing mixed numbers together

Example: $1\frac{1}{2} \div 1\frac{1}{4}$

There are two steps required to work out the division of mixed numbers.

Step1: Convert both mixed numbers into fractions as before

Step 2: Multiply the fractions together but invert the second one.

$$1\frac{1}{2} \div 1\frac{1}{4} = \frac{3}{2} \div \frac{5}{4} = \frac{3}{2} \times \frac{4}{5} = \frac{12}{10} = 1\frac{2}{10} = 1\frac{1}{5}$$

Chapter 6: Proportions and ratios

Although proportion and ratio are related they are not the same thing – see example below for clarification.

Example: In a class there are 15 girls and 10 boys. The **ratio of girls to boys is** 15:10, or 3:2, (divide both 15 and 10 by 5) and the **proportion of girls in the class** is 15 out of 25, $\frac{15}{25}$ which simplifies to $\frac{3}{5}$

Questions based on proportions and ratios

Example 1

In a class of 27 pupils, 9 go home for lunch. What is the proportion of pupils in this class that have lunch at school?

Since 9 out of 27 pupils go home, this means 18 pupils have lunch at school.

As a proportion this is 18 out of 27 or $\frac{18}{27}$ which simplifies to $\frac{2}{3}$

Example 2: In a certain work place the ratio of males to females is 2: 3. There are 250 workers altogether. How many of these are male?

Step 1: Find out the total number of parts. You can do this by adding up the ratio parts together. E.g. 2:3 means there are (2+3) = 5 parts altogether. This means 1 part = one fifth of 250 workers = 50 workers.

Step 2: Since the ratio of male to female is 2:3, there are 2×50 males and 3×50 females

The number of males in this workplace =2×50 = 100

Example 3:

$100 is divided in the ratio 1: 4 how much is the bigger part?

The total number of parts that $100 is divided into is 5 (to find the number of parts simply add the numbers in the ratio, which in this case is 1 and 4)

Clearly, 1 part equals $20 (100 divided by 5), so 4 parts is equal to $80. This is the required bigger part.

Example 4:

$1500 is divided in the ratio of 3 :5 :7

Find out how much the smallest part is worth?

Clearly $1500 is divided into a total of 15 Parts

So each part is worth $100 ($1500 divided by 15)

So 3 parts (this is the smallest part) equals $300

Example 5:

Two lengths are in the ratio 3: 5. If the first length is 150m what is the second length?

If the ratio is 3: 5 then the lengths are in the ratio 150: n (where n is the second length)

We now need to determine n. We can see that 150 is 50 times 3.

So, n (which is the second length) must be 50 times 5, which equals 250m.

Example 6:

As we have seen, sometimes ratios are expressed in ways, which may not be the simplest form. Consider 5 : 10

(a) You can re-write 5 : 10 as 1 : 2 (divide both sides by 5)

(b) 4 : 10 can be re-written as 2 : 5

(c) 8 : 60 can be re-written as 4 : 30 which simplifies to 2 : 15

(d) 15 : 36 simplifies to 5 : 12 (divide both sides by 3)

Increasing & decreasing ratios

Example 1: A small building took 10 people 8 days to build. How long would it take 4 people to build?

Method: Time taken for 10 people = 8 days

So, time taken by 1 person would be 80 days

Hence, time taken by 4 people = 80÷4 = 20 days

Example 2: A recipe for a dessert for 4 people needs $\frac{3}{4}$ tablespoons of sugar. How many tablespoons of sugar do you need for 14 people?

Method: One person needs 3/4 ÷4 tablespoons of sugar = $\frac{3}{4} \times \frac{1}{4} = \frac{3}{16}$

So the amount of sugar needed for 14 people = $\frac{3}{16} \times \frac{14}{1} = \frac{42}{16} = \frac{21}{8} = 2\frac{5}{8}$

tablespoons, or **just over two and half tablespoons** full of sugar

Example 3: A team of 10 people can deliver 6000 leaflets in a residential estate in 4 hours. How long does it take 6 people to deliver these leaflets?

Method: 1 person will take 10 times as long or 4×10 = 40 hours

This means 6 people will take 40÷6 =20 ÷3 = $6\frac{2}{3}$ hours = 6 hours and 40 minutes.

(Since 1/3 of an hour = 20 minutes)

Scales and ratios

Consider that you are reading a map and the scale ratio is 1: 100000

(This means for every one cm on the map the actual distance is 100000 cm or, put another way every one cm on the map, the distance = 1000 m (divide 100000 by 100 to get the result in metres. Now, 1000 m = 1km (divide 1000 by 1000 to get 1 since 1km =1000m)

(Scales can also be used in other areas such as architectural drawings)

Question based on scales

I note that the map I am using has a scale of 1: 25000. The distance between the two places I am interested in is 12cm. What is the actual distance in km?

Method: 12 cm on the map corresponds to 12 x 25000 = 300x 1000 =300000cm

=3000m = 3km. (300000 /100 to convert to metres = 3000 m, now divide 3000 by 1000 to convert to km). Hence the distance between the two places is 3km

---

Conversions

Conversions are often useful in changing currencies for example from pounds to dollars or euros and vice-versa. It is also useful to convert distances from miles to kilometers or weights from kilograms to pounds and so on.

Basically a conversion involves changing information from one unit of measurement to another. Consider some examples below:

Question based on conversions

Example 1:

I go to France with £150 and convert this into Euros at 1.2 Euros to a pound.

(1) How many Euros do I get? **(2)** I am left with 39 Euros when I get back home. The exchange rate remains the same. How many pounds do I get back?

Method: (1) Since 1 pound = 1.2 Euros, I get 150 × 1.2 =180 Euros in total.

(2) When I get back I change 39 Euros back into pounds. This time I need to divide 39 by 1.2

So 39÷1.2 =32.5. This means I get back £32.50

Example 2

The formula for changing kilometers to miles is given by:

$M = \dfrac{5}{8} \times K$. Use this formula to convert 68 kilometers to miles

Method: substitute **K** with 68 and multiply by $\dfrac{5}{8}$

This means $M = \dfrac{5}{8} \times 68$. Using a calculator this comes to 42.5 miles

It is worth reviewing some common Metric and Imperial Measures as shown below

Metric Measures

1000 Millilitres (ml) =1 Litre(l)

100 Centilitres (cl) =1 Litre (l)

10ml =1 cl

1 Centimetre (cm) =10 Millimetres (mm)

1 Metre (m) = 100 cm

1 Kilometre (km) =1000 m

1 Kilogram (kg) =1000 grams (g)

Imperial Measurements

1 foot = 12 inches

1 yard = 3 feet

1 pound = 16 ounces

1 stone = 14 pounds (lb)

1 gallon = 8 pints

1 inch = 2.54 cm (approximately)

Question on conversions

A ramblers' group goes on a walking tour whilst in the South of France. They walk from Perpignan to Canet Plage which is approximately 11 km away. After a lunch break and some time on the beach, they walk back to Perpignan. How many miles in total do they walk on that day? (You are given that 8 km is approximately equal to 5 miles.) Give your answer as a decimal.

Method: Total distance walked = 22Km (11 + 11). To convert this into miles we have to multiply 22 by 5 and then divide by 8 (Since 8 km = 5 miles)

That is $22 \times \dfrac{5}{8}$ =13.75 miles (simply multiply 22 by 5 and divide the answer by 8)

(Remember, use of calculator would be allowed for this type of question)

Chapter 7: Weighted Averages & Formulae

When two or more sets of data are combined together and some are more important than others, then different weightings are given. The weighted mean is then worked out appropriately as shown in the examples below:

Example 1:

In a particular subject the coursework carries a weight of 0.3 and the exam mark carries a weight of 0.7

Calculate the overall percentage result if a pupil got 60% for the coursework and 50% for the exam.

The percentage result is 60X0.3 + 50X0.7 = 18 +35 = 53%

Example 2

A pupil achieved the following marks in three tests

Test 1: 55 marks

Test 2: 60 marks

Test 3: 12 marks

The formula used by the head of maths to work the weighted average for all three tests combined was:

$$\text{Overall weighted average} = \frac{\text{Test1} \times 60}{100} + \frac{\text{Test2} \times 20}{60} + \text{Test3}$$

Using this formula we can work out the overall weighted score as:

$$\frac{55 \times 60}{100} + \frac{60 \times 20}{60} + 12$$

This works out to 33 + 20 +12 = 65 marks

Formula

A formula describes the relationship between two or more variables. Consider a simple case first.

Example 1: A company pays 40p per mile and certain meal expenses when their sales employees visit clients. The cost of claiming mileage is calculated using the formula given, payable at 40p per mile and a fixed cost of £25. The formula is C = M× 0.4 + 25, where C represents the cost in pounds payable to the employee by the company.

So for example if an employee has to travel 40 miles from her home to the client, the employee can claim 80 miles altogether for the journey to the client and back + £25 as shown below by the formula.

Using the formula we have C = 0.4×80 + 25 = 32 + 25 = £57

(Explanation of working out: Using BIDMAS we multiply before adding. So 0.4×80 =32, finally add 32 and 25 together to get 57)

Example 2: The formula for working out time taken is given by T = D÷S

Calculate the time taken to cover 90 miles if I travel at 60mph?

Time taken, T= D÷S, so T = 90÷60 = 9÷6 =3÷ 2 = 1.5 hours or 1 hour and 30 minutes.

Example 3

The formula for converting the temperature from Celsius to Fahrenheit is given by the formula: $F = \frac{9}{5}C + 32$ (where C is the temperature in degrees Centigrade)

If the temperature is 10 degrees Celsius then what is the equivalent temperature in Fahrenheit?

Using the formula $F = \frac{9}{5}C + 32$, and substituting 10 in place of C, we have $F = \frac{9}{5} \times 10 + 32 = \frac{90}{5} + 32 = 18 + 32 = 50$. Hence, 10 degrees centigrade = 50 degrees Fahrenheit

Explanation of working out above: Remember we multiply and divide before adding and subtracting. There are no brackets to worry about. When working out $\frac{9}{5}$ × 10 +32, multiply 9 by 10 to get 90, divide this by 5 to get 18, finally add 18 and 32 together to get 50

Example 4: Convert 68 degrees Fahrenheit to degrees Celsius. The formula for converting the temperature from Fahrenheit to Celsius is given by: $C=\frac{5}{9}(F-32)$. To change 68 degrees Fahrenheit to degrees Celsius we can substitute for F in the formula $C=\frac{5}{9}(F-32)$, $C = C=\frac{5}{9}(68-32)$. $=5 \times 36/9 = 5 \times 4 =20$

Hence, 68 degrees Fahrenheit =20 degrees Celsius

Explanation of the working out above: Using BIDMAS we work out the bracket first. This gives us 68-32 =36. We now divide this by 9 and multiply by 5. Clearly 36÷9 =4 and finally 5×4 =20)

Chapter 8: Speed Distance Time Practice Tests

Some of the questions may seem very easy, but remember it is how accurately and quickly you can do it that is important. Try and get at least 15 out of 20 questions correct in each test. Allow yourself no more than 10 minutes for each test. You may use paper and pencil where necessary, but no calculators are allowed.

Practice Test1

(1) Calculate the distance you would travel if were driving at 30mph for 2 hours?

(2) Calculate the distance you would travel if were driving at 60mph for 3 hours?

(3) Calculate the distance you would travel if were driving at 30mph for 2.5 hours?

(4) What is the average speed of an aircraft if it travels 240 miles in 30 minutes?

(5) What is the average speed of my plane if I travel 255 miles in 30 minutes?

(6) What is the average speed of my car if I travel 200 miles in 5 hours?

(7) What is the time taken to travel 30 miles if my average speed is 60mph?

(8) What is the time taken to travel 45 miles if my average speed is 60 mph?

(9) What is the time taken to travel 90 miles if my average speed is 60 mph?

(10) What is the time taken to travel 150 miles if my average speed is 60 mph?

(11) What is my speed if travel 56 miles in 2 hours?

(12) At 144 mph how long does it take to travel 12 miles?

(13) At 14 mph how far do you travel in 1 hour?

(14) At 48 mph how long does it take me to travel 64 miles?

(15) At 12 mph how far do I travel in 1 hour and 45 minutes?

(16) At 130 mph how far do I travel in 30 minutes?

(17) At 30 mph how far do you travel in 1 hour and 30 minutes?

(18) What is my speed if I cover 8 miles in 24 minutes?

(19) What is my speed if I cover 60 miles in $1\frac{1}{4}$ hours?

(20) At 18 mph how far do I travel in 10 minutes?

Practice Test 2

(1) Calculate the distance you would travel if were driving at 35mph for 2 hours?

(2) Calculate the distance you would travel if were driving at 75mph for 2 hours?

(3) Calculate the distance you would travel if were driving at 40mph for 2.5 hours?

(4) What is the average speed of an aircraft if it travels 220 miles in 30 minutes?

(5) What is the average speed of my plane if I travel 260 miles in 30 minutes?

(6) What is the time taken to travel 40 miles if my average speed is 80mph?

(7) What is the time taken to travel 40 miles if my average speed is 120 mph?

(8) What is the time taken to travel 90 miles if my average speed is 30 mph?

(9) What is the time taken to travel 20 miles if my average speed is 60 mph?

(10) What is my speed if I travel 58 miles in 2 hours?

(11) At 72 mph how long does it take to travel 12 miles?

(12) At 16.5 mph how far do you travel in 1 hour?

(13) At 16 mph how long does it take me to travel 48 miles?

(14) At 16 mph how far do I travel in 1 hour and 45 minutes?

(15) At 170 mph how far do I travel in 30 minutes?

(16) What is my speed if I cover 12 miles in 24 minutes?

(17) What is my speed if I cover 80 miles in $1\frac{1}{4}$ hours?

(18) At 18 mph how far do I travel in 10 minutes?

(19) What speed covers 180 km in $2\frac{1}{4}$ hours?

(20) At 36 km/h how far do you travel in 45 minutes?

Practice Test 3

(1) At 150 mph how much time does it take to cover 75 miles?

(2) To cover 60 km in 5 minutes, what speed do I have to travel?

(3) At 44 km/h what distance will I cover in 45 minutes?

(4) What speed covers 81 km in $2\frac{1}{4}$ hours?

(5) At 64 km/h how far do you travel in 45 minutes?

(6) At 270 km/h how far do you far do you travel in 40 minutes?

(7) At 32 km/h how long does it take to travel 80 km?

(8) At 64km/h how long does it take to travel 128km?

(9) What speed covers 90km in 20 minutes?

(10) What speed covers 48km in 1 hour?

(11) At 63 km/h how far do you travel in 40 minutes?

(12) What speed covers 90 km in 1 hour and 40 minutes?

(13) At 60 mph how far do you travel in 20 minutes?

(14) At 360 mph how long does it take to travel 90 miles?

(15) At 38 mph how far do you travel in $2\frac{1}{2}$ hours?

(16) What speed covers 12 miles in 15 minutes?

(17) At 40 mph how far do you travel in 1 hour and 12 minutes?

(18) What speed covers 102 miles in 30 minutes?

(19) What speed covers 27 miles in 40 minutes?

(20) At 180 mph how long does it take to travel 45 miles?

Practice Test 4

(1) Calculate the distance you would travel if were driving at 38mph for 2 hours?

(2) Calculate the distance you would travel if were driving at 60mph for $2\frac{3}{4}$ hours?

(3) What is the average speed of an aircraft if I travel 235 miles in 30 minutes?

(4) What is the average speed of my plane if I travel 270 miles in 45 minutes?

(5) What is the average speed of my car if I travel 240 miles in 4 hours?

(6) What is the time taken to travel 45 miles if my average speed is 60mph?

(7) What is the time taken to travel 40 miles if my average speed is 120 mph?

(8) What is the time taken to travel 120 miles if my average speed is 80 mph?

(9) What is the time taken to travel 180 miles if my average speed is 60 mph?

(10) What is my speed if I travel 123 miles in 3 hours?

(11) At 144 mph how long does it take to travel 12 miles?

(12) At 91 mph how far do you travel in 1 hour?

(13) At 48 mph how long does it take me to travel 72 miles?

(14) At 24 mph how far do I travel in 1 hour and 45 minutes?

(15) At 120 mph how far do I travel in 20 minutes?

(16) At 50 mph how far do you travel in 1 hour and 30 minutes?

(17) What is my speed if I cover 16 miles in 24 minutes?

(18) What is my speed if I cover 80 miles in $1\frac{1}{4}$ hours?

(19) At 15 mph how far do I travel in 20 minutes?

(20) Calculate the distance you would travel if were driving at 36mph for 2.5 hours?

Practice Test 5

(1) Calculate the distance you would travel if were driving at 77 mph for 2 hours?

(2) Calculate the distance you would travel if were driving at 66 mph for $1\frac{1}{2}$ hours?

(3) Calculate the distance you would travel if were driving at 38 mph for 2.5 hours?

(4) What is the average speed of an aircraft if I travel 280 miles in 30 minutes?

(5) What is the average speed of my plane if I travel 275 miles in 30 minutes?

(6) What is the average speed of my car if I travel 560 miles in 8 hours?

(7) What is the time taken to travel 25 miles if my average speed is 75 mph?

(8) What is the time taken to travel 65 miles if my average speed is 130 mph?

(9) What is the time taken to travel 40 miles if my average speed is 60 mph?

(10) What is the time taken to travel 120 miles if my average speed is 90 mph?

(11) What is my speed if travel 63 miles in 3 hours?

(12) At 144 mph how long does it take to travel 24 miles?

(13) At 16.5 mph how far do you travel in 1 hour?

(14) At 48 mph how long does it take me to travel 72 miles?

(15) At 48 mph how far do I travel in 1 hour and 45 minutes?

(16) At 120 mph how far do I travel in 10 minutes?

(17) At 70 mph how far do you travel in 2 hours and 30 minutes?

(18) What is my speed if I cover 24 miles in 48 minutes?

(19) What is my speed if I cover 120 miles in $1\frac{1}{4}$ hours?

(20) At 64 mph how far do I travel in 15 minutes?

Answers to practice Test 1

(1) Answer = **60 miles**

Method: Distance = Speed × Time = 30×2 = 60

(2) Answer = 180 miles

Method: Distance= Speed × Time = 60×3 = 180

(3) Answer = 75 miles

Method: Distance = Speed × Time = 30×2.5 = 75

(4) Answer = 480 mph

Method: Speed = Distance ÷ Time = $240 \div \frac{1}{2} = 480$

(5) **Answer:** = 510 mph

Method: Speed = Distance ÷ Time = $255 \div \frac{1}{2} = 510$ miles

(6) Answer:=40 mph

Method: Speed **=** Distance ÷ Time =200÷5 = 40 miles

(7) Answer:= 0.5 hours or 30 minutes

Method: Time = Distance ÷ Speed = 30÷60 = 0.5 hours = 30 minutes

(8) Answer: = 45 minutes

Method: Time = Distance ÷ Speed = $45 \div 60 = \frac{45}{60}$ (divide top and bottom of this fraction by 15). So $\frac{45}{60} = \frac{3}{4}$ hours = 45 minutes

(9) Answer = 1.5 hours or 1 hour and 30 minutes

Method: Time = Distance ÷ Speed = 90÷60 = 1.5hrs = 1hour 30 minutes

(10) Answer = 2.5 hours or 2 hours and 30 minutes

Method: Time = Distance ÷ Speed = 150÷60 which simplifies to 15÷6 =2.5 hours or 2 hours and 30 minutes

(11) Answer = 28 mph

Method: Speed = Distance ÷ Time = 56÷2 = 28 mph

(12) Answer = 5 minutes

Method: Time = Distance ÷ Speed = 12÷144 = 1÷12 = $\frac{1}{12}$ hour = 5 minutes

(13) Answer = 14miles

Method: Distance = Speed ×Times = 14 ×1 = 14 miles

(14) Answer = 1 hour 20 minutes

Method: Time = Distance ÷ Speed = 64÷48 which simplifies to 8÷6 =4÷3 = $1\frac{1}{3}$ hours = 1 hour 20 minutes

(15) 21 miles

Method: Distance = Speed ×Time = 12 ×$1\frac{3}{4}$ = 12×1 + 12×$\frac{3}{4}$ =12 + 9 =21 miles

(16) Answer = 65 miles

Method: Distance × Time = 130 × 0.5 = 65 miles

(17) Answer = 45 miles

Method: Distance = Speed × Time = 30 × 1.5 = 45 miles

(18) Answer = 20mph

Method: Speed = Distance ÷ Time = 8 ÷ 0.4 = 20 mph (since 8 ÷ 0.4 is the same as 80 ÷ 4 = 20

(Note that 24 minutes = $\frac{24}{60}$ hours. This simplifies to $\frac{2}{5}$ hours = 0.4 hours (dividing top and bottom of $\frac{24}{60}$ by 12 gives $\frac{2}{5}$)

(19) Answer = 48 mph

Method: Speed = Distance ÷ Time = $60 \div 1\frac{1}{4} = 60 \div \frac{5}{4} = 60 \times \frac{4}{5} = \frac{240}{5}$ = 48mph

(20) Answer = 3 miles

Method: Distance = Speed × Time = $18 \times \frac{10}{60} = 18 \times \frac{1}{6} = \frac{18}{6}$ = 3 miles

Answers to practice Test 2

(1) Answer = **70 miles**

Method: Distance = Speed × Time = 35×2 = 70

(2) Answer = 150 miles

Method: Distance = Speed × Time = 75×2 = 150

(3) Answer = 100 miles

Method: Distance = Speed × Time = 40×2.5 = 100

(4) Answer = 440 mph

Method: Speed = Distance ÷ Time = $220 \div \frac{1}{2} = 440$

(5) Answer: = 520 mph

Method: Speed = Distance ÷ Time = $260 \div \frac{1}{2} = 520$ miles

(6) Answer: = 30 minutes

Method: Time = Distance ÷ Speed = 40÷80 = 0.5 hours = 30 minutes

(7) Answer: = 20 minutes

Method: Time = Distance ÷ Speed = $40 \div 120 = \frac{1}{3}$ hour = 20 minutes

(8) Answer: = 3 hours

Method: Time = Distance ÷ Speed = 90÷30 = 3 hours

(9) Answer = 20 minutes

Method: Time = Distance ÷ Speed = 20÷60 = $\frac{1}{3}$ hour = 20 minutes

(10) Answer = 29 mph

Method: Speed = Distance ÷ Time = 58÷2 = 29 mph

(11) Answer = 10 minutes

Method: Time = Distance ÷ Speed = 12÷72 which simplifies to 1÷6 = $\frac{1}{6}$ hour = 10 minutes

(12) Answer = 16.5 miles

Method: Distance = Speed × Time = 16.5×1 = 16.5 miles

(13) Answer = 3 hours

Method: Time = Distance ÷ Speed = 48 ÷16 = 3 hours

(14) Answer = 28 miles

Method: Distance = Speed × Time = 16×$1\frac{3}{4}$ =16×1 +16× $\frac{3}{4}$ =16 + 12 = 28 miles

(15) 85 miles

Method: Distance = Speed ×Time = 170 ×0.5 = 85 miles

(16) Answer = 30 mph

Method: Speed = Distance÷ Time = 12 ×0.4 = 30 mph

(Note that 24 minutes = $\frac{24}{60}$ hours simplifies to $\frac{2}{5}$ hours = 0.4 hours (dividing top and bottom of $\frac{24}{60}$ by 12 gives $\frac{2}{5}$)

(17) Answer = 64 mph

Method: Speed = Distance ÷ Time = $80 \div 1\frac{1}{4} = 80 \div \frac{5}{4} = 80 \times \frac{4}{5} = \frac{320}{5} = 64$

(18) Answer = 3 miles

Method: Distance = Speed × Time = $18 \times \frac{1}{6} = \frac{18}{6} = 3$ miles

(19) Answer = 80 km/hour

Method: Speed = Distance ÷ Time = $180 \div 2\frac{1}{4} = 180 \div \frac{9}{4} = 180 \times \frac{4}{9} = \frac{720}{9} = 80$

(20) Answer = 27 km

Method: Distance = Speed × Time = $36 \times \frac{3}{4} = = \frac{108}{4} = 27$ km
(Note that 45 minutes = $\frac{45}{60}$ (divide top and bottom by 15) this simplifies to $\frac{3}{4}$ hours

Answers to practice Test 3

(1) Answer = **30 minutes or $\frac{1}{2}$ hour**

   Method: Method: Time = Distance ÷ Speed = 75÷150 = 0.5 hours = 30 minutes

(2) Answer = 720km/hour

   Method: Speed = Distance ÷ Time = $60 \div \frac{1}{12}$ (5 minutes = $\frac{1}{12}$ of an hour). Hence, $60 \div \frac{1}{12} = 60 \times \frac{12}{1} = \frac{720}{1} = 720$ km/hour

(3) Answer = 33 km

   Method: Distance = Speed × Time = $44 \times \frac{3}{4} = 33$ km

(4) Answer = 36 km/hour

   Method: Speed = Distance ÷ Time = $81 \div 2\frac{1}{4} = 81 \div \frac{9}{4} = 81 \times \frac{4}{9}$ = 36km/hour

(5) Answer: = 48 km

   Method: Distance = Speed × Time = $64 \times \frac{3}{4} = 48$ km

(6) Answer: = 180 km

   Method: Distance = Speed × Time = $270 \times \frac{2}{3} = 180$ km

(7) Answer: = 2 hours 30 minutes or $2\frac{1}{2}$ hours

   Method: Time = Distance ÷ Speed = $80 \div 32 = \frac{80}{32} = \frac{10}{4} = 2\frac{1}{2}$ hrs

(8) Answer: = 2 hours

Method: Time = Distance ÷ Speed = 128÷64 = 2 hours

(9) Answer = 270 km/hr

Method: Speed = Distance ÷ Time = $90 \div \frac{1}{3} = 90 \times \frac{3}{1} = \frac{270}{1} = 270$ km/hr

(10) Answer = 48km/hr

Method: Speed = Distance ÷ Time = 48÷1 = 48 km/hr

(11) Answer = 42km/hr

Method: Distance = Speed × Time = $63 \times \frac{2}{3} = \frac{126}{3} = 42$

(12) Answer = 54km/hr

Method: Speed = Distance ÷ Time = $90 \div 1\frac{2}{3} = 90 \div \frac{5}{3} = 90 \times \frac{3}{5} = 54$ km/hr

(13) Answer = 20 miles

Method: Distance = Speed × Time = $60 \times \frac{1}{3} = \frac{60}{3} = 20$ miles

(14) Answer = 15 minutes or $\frac{1}{4}$ hour

Method: Time = Distance ÷ Speed = $90 \div 360 = \frac{1}{4}$ hour = 15 minutes

(15) 95 miles

Method: Distance = Speed × Time = 38 × 2.5 = 2×38 + 0.5×38 = 76 + 19 = 95 miles

(16) Answer = 48 mph

76

Method: Speed = Distance ÷ Time = $12 \div \frac{15}{60} = 12 \div \frac{1}{4} = 12 \times \frac{4}{1} = 48$ mph

(Note that 15 minutes = $\frac{15}{60}$ hours which simplifies to $\frac{1}{4}$ hours)

(17) Answer = 48 miles

Method: Distance = Speed × Time = $40 \times 1\frac{1}{5} = 40 \times \frac{6}{5} = \frac{240}{5} = 48$ miles

(18) Answer = 204 mph/hour

Method: Speed = Distance ÷ Time = $102 \div \frac{1}{2} = 102 \times 2 = 204$ mph

(19) Answer = 40.5 mph

Method: Speed = Distance ÷ Time = $27 \div \frac{2}{3} = 27 \times \frac{3}{2} = \frac{81}{2} = 40.5$ mph

(20) Answer = 15 minutes or $\frac{1}{4}$ hour

Method: Time = Distance ÷ Speed = $45 \div 180 = \frac{45}{180} = \frac{1}{4}$ hour = 15 minutes

Answers to practice Test 4

(1) Answer = **76 miles**

Method: Distance = Speed × Time = 38×2 = 76 miles

(2) Answer = **165 miles**

Method: Distance = Speed × Time = $60 \times 2\frac{3}{4}$ = 60×2 + 60×$\frac{3}{4}$
= 120 + 45 = 165 miles

(3) Answer = **470 mph**

Method: Speed = Distance ÷ Time = $235 \div \frac{1}{2}$ = 470

(4) Answer = **360 mph**

Method: Speed = Distance ÷ Time = $270 \div \frac{3}{4}$ = 270 × $\frac{4}{3}$
= 90×4 = 360 mph

(5) Answer: = **60 mph**

Method: Speed = Distance ÷ Time = 240÷4 = 60 mph

(6) Answer: = **45 minutes or $\frac{3}{4}$ hours**

Method: Time = Distance ÷ Speed = 45÷60 = $\frac{45}{60}$ = $\frac{3}{4}$ hours = 45 minutes

(7) Answer: = **20 minutes**

Method: Time = Distance ÷ Speed = 40÷120 = $\frac{40}{120}$ = $\frac{1}{3}$ hours = 20 minutes

(8) Answer: = **1 hour 30 minutes or $1\frac{1}{2}$ hours**

Method: Time = Distance ÷ Speed = 120÷80 = $\frac{120}{80}$ (divide top and bottom of this fraction by 40). So $\frac{120}{80} = \frac{3}{2} = 1.5$ hours = 1 hour 30 minutes

(9) Answer = 3 hours

Method: Time = Distance ÷ Speed = 180÷60 = 3 hours

(10) Answer = 41 mph

Method: Speed = Distance ÷ Time = 123÷3 = 41 mph

(11) Answer = 5 minutes

Method: Time = Distance ÷ Speed = 12÷144 = $\frac{12}{144} = \frac{1}{12}$ of an hour = 5 minutes

(12) Answer = 91 miles

Method: Distance = Speed ×Times = 91×1= 91 miles

(13) Answer = 1 hour 30 minutes or $1\frac{1}{2}$ hours

Method: Time = Distance ÷ Speed = 72÷48 = $\frac{72}{48} = \frac{9}{6} = 1\frac{3}{6}$ =1.5 hours = 1 hour 30 minutes

(14) Answer = 42 miles

Method: Distance = Speed ×Times = 24×$1\frac{3}{4}$ which simplifies to 24 + $\frac{3}{4}$ ×24 = 24 + 18 =42 miles

(15) 40 miles

Method: Distance = Speed ×Time = 120 ×$\frac{1}{3} = \frac{120}{3}$ =40 miles

(16) Answer = 75 miles

Method: Distance = Speed × Time = 50 ×1.5 = 75 miles

(17) Answer = 40 mph

Method: Speed = Distance ÷ Time = $16 \div \frac{2}{5} = 16 \times \frac{5}{2} = \frac{80}{2}$ = 40mph

(18) Answer = 64 mph

Method: Speed = Distance ÷ Time = $80 \div 1\frac{1}{4} = 80 \div \frac{5}{4} = 80 \times \frac{4}{5} = \frac{320}{5}$
=64 mph

(19) Answer = 5 miles

Method: Distance = Speed ×Time = $15 \times \frac{1}{3} = \frac{15}{3}$ = 5 miles

(20) Answer = 90 miles

Method: Distance = Speed ×Time = 36 × 2.5= 36×2 + 36×0.5 = 72 +18 = 90 miles

Answers to practice Test 5

(1) Answer **= 154 miles**

   Method: Distance = Speed × Time = 77×2 = 154

(2) Answer = 99 miles

   Method: Distance= Speed × Time = 66×1.5 = 66 + 33 =99 miles

(3) Answer = 95 miles

   Method: Distance = Speed × Time = 38×2.5 = 38×2 + 38×0.5 = 76 +19 = 95 miles

(4) Answer = 560 mph

   Method: Speed = Distance ÷ Time = $280 \div \frac{1}{2} = 280 \times \frac{2}{1}$ = 560 mph

(5) Answer: = 550 mph

   Method: Speed = Distance ÷ Time = $275 \div \frac{1}{2}$ = 540 mph

(6) Answer: =70 mph

   Method: Speed = Distance ÷ Time =560÷8 = 70 mph

(7) Answer:= 20 minutes

   Method: Time = Distance ÷ Speed = 25÷75 = $\frac{25}{75} = \frac{1}{3}$ hour = 20 minutes

(8) Answer: = 30 minutes or $\frac{1}{2}$ hour

Method: Time = Distance ÷ Speed = 65÷130 = $\frac{65}{130}$ (divide top and bottom of this fraction by 65). So $\frac{65}{130} = \frac{1}{2}$ hour = 30 minutes

(9) Answer = 40 minutes

Method: Time = Distance ÷ Speed = 40÷60 = $\frac{40}{60} = \frac{2}{3}$ hour = 40 minutes

(10) Answer = 1 hour 20 minutes

Method: Time = Distance ÷ Speed = 120÷90 which simplifies to 12÷9 = 4÷3 = $1\frac{1}{3}$ hours = 1 hour 20 minutes

(11) Answer = 21 mph

Method: Speed = Distance ÷ Time = 63÷3 = 21 mph

(12) Answer = 10 minutes

Method: Time = Distance ÷ Speed = 24÷144 = 2÷12 = $\frac{1}{6}$ hour = 10 minutes

(13) Answer = 16.5 miles

Method: Distance = Speed ×Times = 16.5 ×1 = 16.5 miles

(14) Answer = 1 hour 30 minutes or $1\frac{1}{2}$ hours

Method: Time = Distance ÷ Speed = 72÷48 which simplifies to 6÷4 =3÷2 = $1\frac{1}{2}$ hour = 1 hour 30 minutes

(15) 84 miles

Method: Distance = Speed ×Time = 48 ×$1\frac{3}{4}$ = 48×1 + 48×$\frac{3}{4}$ = 48 +36 = 84 miles

(16) Answer = 20 miles

Method: Distance × Time = $120 \times \frac{1}{6}$ = 20 miles (Note 10 minutes = $\frac{1}{6}$ hour)

(17) Answer = 175 miles

Method: Distance = Speed × Time = 70×2.5 = 70×2 + 70×0.5 = 140 + 35 = 175 miles

(18) Answer = 30mph

Method: Speed = Distance ÷ Time = 24÷0.8 = 240÷8 = 30 mph (Note: 48 minutes = $\frac{48}{60}$ hours which simplifies to $\frac{4}{5}$ = 0.8)

(19) Answer = 96 mph

Method: Speed = Distance ÷ Time = $120 \div 1\frac{1}{4} = 120 \div \frac{5}{4} = 120 \times \frac{4}{5} = \frac{480}{5}$ = 96 mph

(20) Answer = 16 miles

Method: Distance = Speed × Time = $64 \times \frac{15}{60} = 64 \times \frac{1}{4} = \frac{64}{4}$ = 16 miles

Time – Distance graphs

Example: A school trip by coach to a heritage site leaves at 1200hrs from the school. The coach arrives at the destination at 1300hrs. It then stops so the pupils can look around the site. Finally after looking around the site it leaves and arrives back at school at 15:30hrs. (1) How long did the coach stop for? (2) What was the average speed on the return journey?

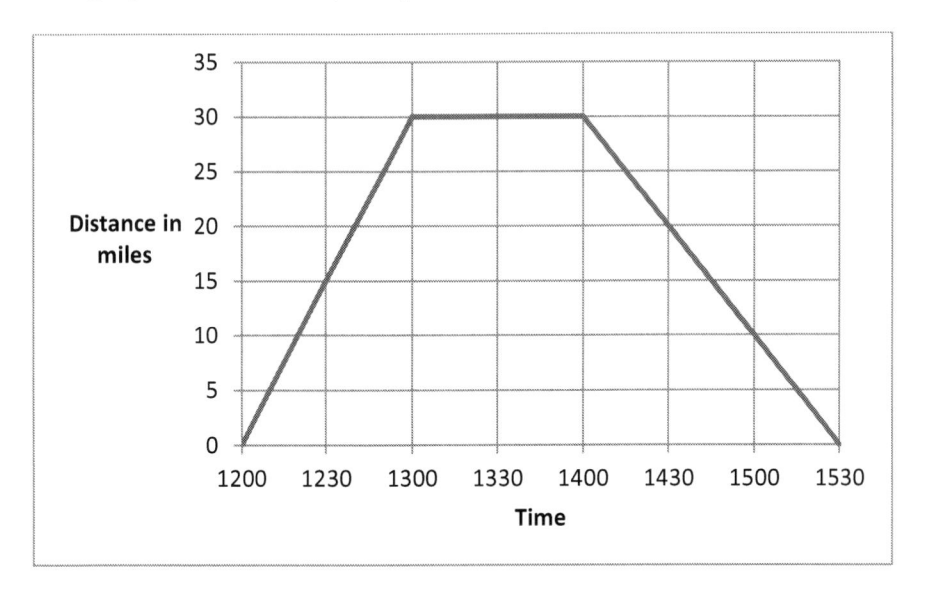

(1) From the distance-time graph above you can see it was stationary from 1300 – 1400hrs, which is 1hr

(Between these time intervals no further distance is covered, so it is stationary – see the vertical axis at 30 miles)

(2) The return journey starts at 1400hrs and ends at school at 1530hrs = 1.5 hrs.

Since $Speed = \frac{Distance}{Time}$, this means speed = 30÷1.5 = 20 mph

You might find the following conversions useful to go through

(Typically the Numerical reasoning test questions give you the conversion formula in the relevant questions)

1 km = 5/8 mile

1 mile = 8/5 km

1 kg = 2.2 lb (approximately)

1 gallon = 4.5 litres (approximately)

1 inch = 2.54 cm (approximately)

Chapter 9: Number Sequences

Many numerical aptitude tests contain questions involving identifying number patterns in order to find the subsequent missing number(s).

Try these questions yourself and see how many you can do. Then check the answers and their rationale.

Complete the following sequences by finding the missing numbers:

(1) 4, 7, 10, 13, ___ , ___
(2) 21, 17, 13, 9, 5, ___ , ___
(3) 18, 9, 4.5, ___ , ___
(4) 0, 1, 1, 2, 3, 5, 8, ___ , ___
(5) 1, 4, 9, 16, 25, ___ , ___
(6) 1, 8, 27, 64, ___ , ___
(7) 17, 12, 7, 2, ___ , ___
(8) 1, 6, 36, 216, ___ , ___
(9) 128, 32, 8, ___ , ___
(10) 36, 49, 64, 81, ___ , ___
(11) 11, 121, 1331, ___ , ___
(12) 81, 729, 6561, ___ , ___
(13) 1, 3, 6, 10, ___ , ___

Answers and their rationale:

(1) 16, 19 (each number increases by a constant value of 3)
(2) 1, -3 (each number decreases by a constant value of 4)
(3) 2.25, 1.125 (each number is half the previous number)
(4) 13, 21 (each number is the sum of the previous two numbers)
(5) 36, 49 (each number is the square of natural numbers, the first number is 1 × 1, the second number is 2 × 2, the third number is 3 × 3, ……the sixth number is 6 × 6, the seventh number is 7 × 7)
(6) 125, 216 (cubes of natural numbers. The first number is 1 × 1 × 1, the second number is 2 × 2 × 2, 3 × 3 × 3, ……5 × 5 × 5, 6 × 6 × 6)
(7) −3, −8 (numbers are decreasing by 5)
(8) 1296, 7776 (each number is 6× the previous number)
(9) 2, 1/2 (each number is a quarter of the previous number)
(10) 100, 121 (square numbers again, the previous number was 9 × 9, then 10 × 10 and finally 11 ×11)
(11) 14641, 161051 (each number is 11× the previous number)
(12) 59049, 531441 (each number is 9× the previous one)

(13) 15, 21 (Triangular numbers, the last difference was 5 and the subsequent 6.)

Finding the Nth term of an arithmetical sequence:

Example 1:

Consider the sequence 2, 4, 6, 8, 10, ___ , ___ , ___ ,

If we want to find a general formula for this sequence we can write it as 2n. 2n is the right answer, since if n=1, we get 2 as the first number. If n=2, we get: 2 × 2 =4 as the second number, if n=4, we get 8 as the fourth number and so on. All we have to do is to substitute the appropriate number for n to get the relevant number in the sequence. So the 50th term is 2 × 50 =100.

Working out formula for sequences:

This time consider a general arithmetical sequence as shown:

a, a +d, a+2d, a +3d, a+4d, a+5d, a+6d, ...

We can see that the second term is a+d

The third term is a+2d

The fourth term is a+3d

The fifth term is a+4d or a +(5-1)d

The sixth term is a+5d or a +(6-1)d

The seventh term is a+6d or a +(7-1)d

So the nth term is a+(n-1)d

You can check to see if this is right by substituting n=1, 2, 3, 4, 5 and so on to the appropriate numbers in the sequence. See example below:

Example: Find the nth term of the arithmetical sequence below:

5, 9, 13, 17, …

This is an arithmetical or linear sequence since the numbers go up by the same constant number. We know the nth term is $a + (n-1)d$

In this case a=5 (This is the first term) d = 4 (this is the common difference between each successive number)

So, the nth term is $5 + (n-1) \times 4 = 5 + 4n - 4 = 4n + 1$,

Chapter 10: Perimeters and Volumes of common shapes

Consider the shapes below:

(1) Rectangle

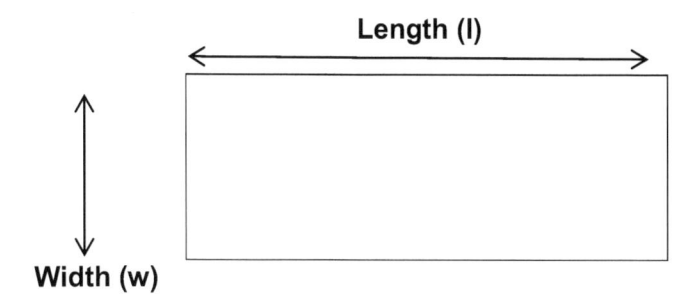

```
            Length (l)
      ←─────────────────→
      ┌─────────────────┐
   ↑  │                 │
   │  │                 │
   ↓  │                 │
      └─────────────────┘
 Width (w)
```

Area of a rectangle = Length × Width or l × w

Perimeter of a rectangle = 2l + 2w (distance around the rectangle)

Note: Area is measured in units squared, e.g. cm^2 or m^2 and perimeter (distance all round a shape) is measured in the appropriate units e.g. cm or m

---

Question based on areas

Example 1: Find the area and perimeter of a rectangle whose length is 12 cm and width is 5cm

Method: Area of a rectangle = l × w = 12 × 5 = 60 cm^2.

Perimeter = 2l + 2w = 2×12 + 2×5 = 24 + 10 = 34 cm. **Note:** For a square the length and width are obviously the same so the formula simplifies to l×l for the area and 4l for the perimeter, where l is the length of each side of the square

Example 2: Find the area of a square whose sides are 1m. Give your answer in cm^2

Area of square in metres squared = 1×1 = 1 m^2, but 1 m = 100cm.

So area in cm^2 = 100×100 = 10000 cm^2

89

(2) Triangle

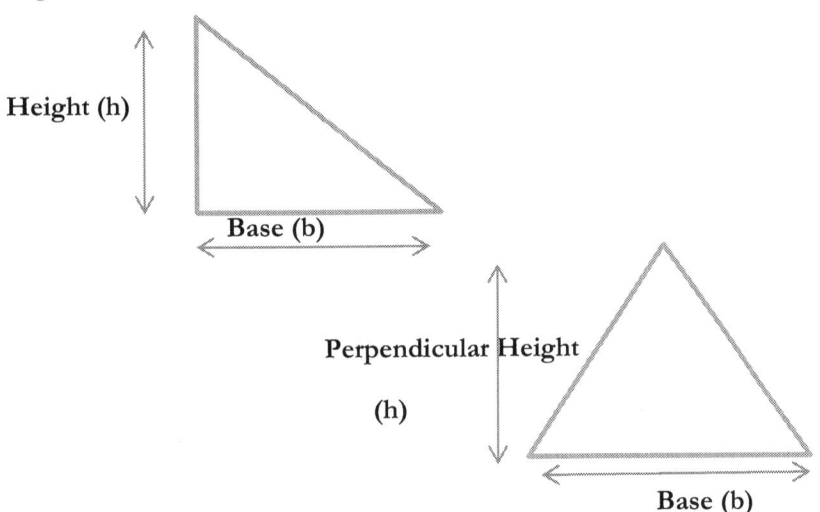

Area of a triangle = $\frac{1}{2}$ × base × height or $\frac{1}{2}$bh (The height is the perpendicular height relative to the base)

Example: Find the area of a triangle whose base is 5m and height is 8m

Method: Area of a triangle = $\frac{1}{2}$ × base × height

Substituting the values for base and height we get Area = $\frac{1}{2}$ × 5 × 8 =

$\frac{1}{2}$ × 40 = 20 m^2

---

(3) Circle

Area of a circle is πr^2 (this means the value of π(pi) multiplied by radius squared)

Circumference of a circle (distance all the way round a circle) = $2\pi r$ or πd

$2\pi r$ = 2 × π(pi)) × radius or π×diameter

Note: Diameter of a circle = 2 × Radius

π = 3.14 (approximately)

(4) Cuboid (or a box)

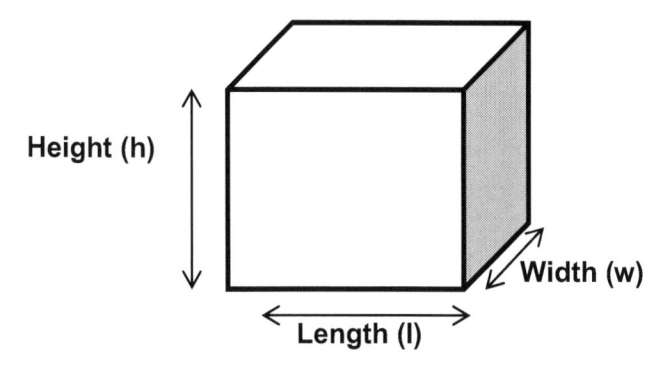

Volume of a cuboid is Height × Length × Width or V = h×l×w (units cubed e.g. cm^3 or m^3, etc)

Example: Find volume of a box whose width =3m, length =5m and height = 6m

Method: Volume of a cuboid (box) = h×l×w = 6×5×3 =30×3 = 90 m^3

Angles

Circle = 360° angle

Straight line = 180°

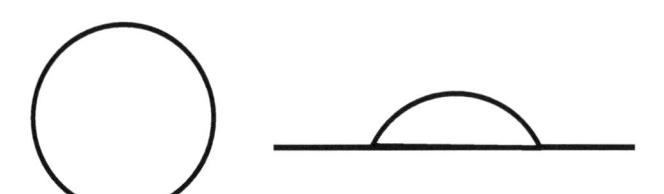

Right angle

90°

Example

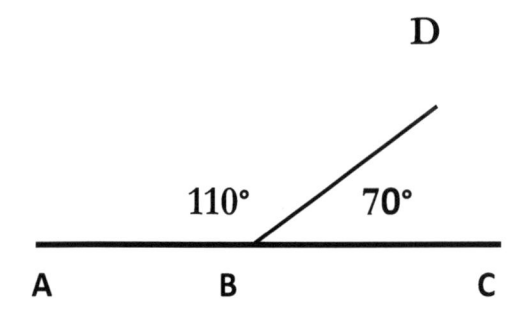

If Angle CBD = 70°. Then angle ABD = 180° – 70° = 110° (Since ABC is a straight line =180°)

Bearings

Bearings are measured clockwise from the north line to the line joining the two points as shown below:

Example: The bearing from A to B is measured clockwise from the North line and in this case is 75°

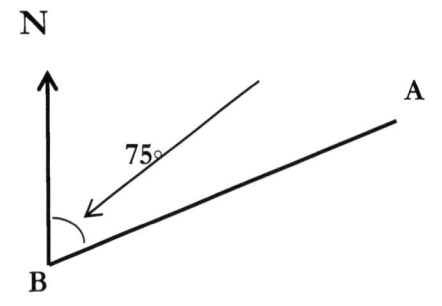

Chapter 11: Data Interpretation

Mean, Median, Mode and Range

First consider the different types of 'averages'.

That is Mean, Median, Mode and Range (You can try to remember these as: MMMR)

Mean (Average) : The sum of the numbers in a data set divided by the number of values in the
Set

Median: The middle number of a data set when listed in order

Mode: The most frequently occurring number or numbers in a data set

Range: The difference between the highest and the smallest numbers in a data set

Example 1:
Find the mean value of the following data set:
2, 7, 1, 1, 7, 8, 9

Method: Find the sum first
2 + 7 + 1 + 1 + 7 + 8 + 9 = 35
Now divide this total by 7, since this is the total number of numbers
So, 35/7 = 5
Hence, the mean value of this data set is 5

Example 2:
Find the median of 3, 7, 1, 8, and 6

Method: First re-order from smallest to biggest, re-writing the numbers we have: 1, 3, 6, 7, 8
Clearly the middle number is 6.
Hence, the median is 6

Example 3:
Find the median of 3, 6, 7, 1, 8 and 5

Method
First re-arrange to get 1, 3, 5, 6, 7, 8

Notice, in this case the middle number is between 5 & 6
So the median is (5 + 6)/2 = 5.5

Example 4:
Find the Range of the data set 3, 5, 7, 1, 8, and 11

Method: Find the difference between the biggest and smallest numbers
So the Range = 11 − 1 = 10

Example 5:
Find the Mode of the following numbers:
1, 4, 4, 4, 7, 8, 9, 9, 11, 12

Method: Find the most frequently occurring number. The most frequently occurring number is 4.
Hence the Mode is 4

Example 6:
Find the mode of 1, 3, 3, 3, 3 5, 5, 5, 5, 8, 8, 9

Method: As before find the most frequently occurring number(s).
Clearly there are two modes here. Both '3' and '5' occur most frequently, the same number of times, so we say this is a bi-modal distribution. That is, a distribution with two modes, namely 3 and 5

Example 1:

The set of data below is the result in a class maths test showing the marks out of 10 for a group of 27 pupils. The teacher wants to find (1) the mode and (2) the mean mark for this test.

Maths marks	No of pupils (frequency)	No. of pupils × maths marks (frequency × marks)	
9	0	0 × 9 = 0	
8	1	1 × 8 = 8	
7	2	2 × 7 = 14	
6	5	5 × 6 = 30	
5	8	8 × 5 = 40	
4	7	7 × 4 = 28	
3	4	4× 3 = 12	
2	0	0 × 2 = 0	
1	0	0 × 1 = 0	
Totals	27	0+8+14+30+40+28+12+0+0=132	

(1) The mode is simply the most frequently occurring mark. In this case it is 5 marks

(Since 8 pupils get this, clearly it is the most common result)

(2) To work out the mean we need to work out the sum of all (pupils × marks) and divide it by the total number of pupils as shown below:

Sum all (pupils × marks) as shown above =132

The total number of pupils who took the test is 27

The mean mark in this test was thus 132 ÷ 27 = 4.9 (to 1 decimal place)

Pie Charts

When data is represented in a circle this is called a pie chart. Basically you need to remember that a full circle or 360 degrees represents all the data (or 100% of the data). Half a circle or 180 degrees represents half the data (or 50% of the data), and similarly 25% of the data is represented by 90 degrees or a quarter of a circle. Essentially, each sector or slice of the pie chart shows the proportion of the total data in that category.

Example 1:

The pie chart below shows the percentage of applicants who got different grades in a psychometric aptitude test when applying for a job in a particular company. The requirement to be short listed for a second interview was to pass with high marks. If 140 applicants took this test how many of them were short listed?

Method: As illustrated the results in this aptitude test for this particular company show that 25% got the required 'high marks' to be short listed for a second

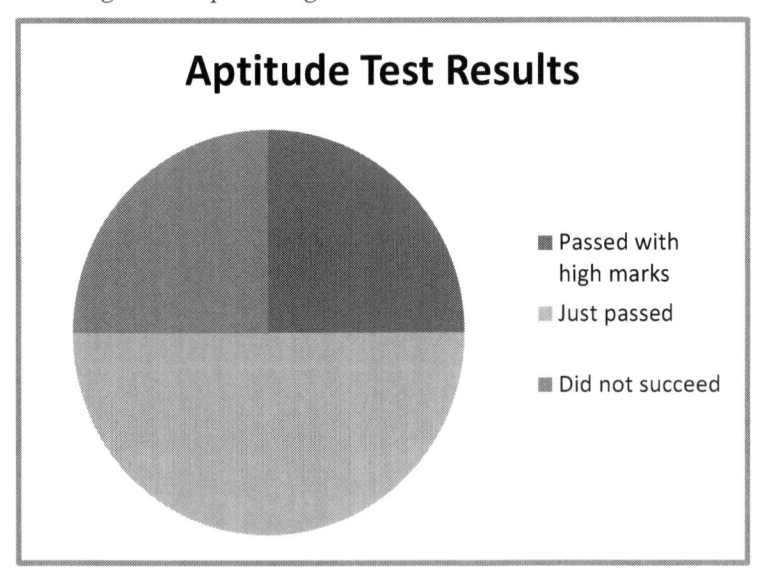

Aptitude Test Results

- Passed with high marks
- Just passed
- Did not succeed

interview. Since a quarter of a circle corresponds to 25%. This means a quarter of the 140 applicants attained this which corresponds to 35 people.

Example 2:

The destination of 120 pupils who leave year 11 in School B in 2012 is represented in the pie chart below. The numbers outside the sectors represent the number of pupils

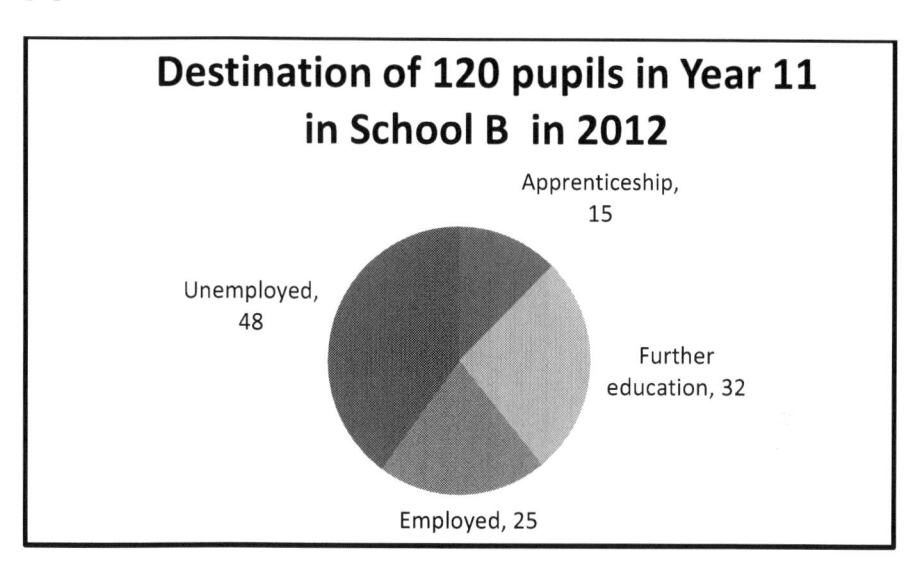

Destination of 120 pupils in Year 11 in School B in 2012

- Apprenticeship, 15
- Unemployed, 48
- Further education, 32
- Employed, 25

(1) What is the percentage of pupils who are unemployed?

Method:

The number of pupils out of 120 that are unemployed is 48. So the percentage of pupils who are unemployed is $\frac{48}{120} \times 100 = \frac{4800}{120} = \frac{480}{12} = 40\%$

(2) What fraction of pupils go on to Further Education?

Method:

The fraction of pupils that go on to further education is $\frac{32}{120} = \frac{8}{30} = \frac{4}{15}$, the fraction representing this in its simplest form is $\frac{4}{15}$

(3) What percentage of pupils is either employed or in apprenticeships? Give your answer to one decimal place?

Method:

Total number of pupils who are either in employment or apprenticeships = 25+15 =40, hence the percentage is $\frac{40}{120} \times 100 = \frac{4}{12} \times 100 = \frac{1}{3} \times 100 = 33.3\%$

Example 3

Key Stage 3 results in English in two adjacent areas A and B are shown in the pie charts below. Area A recorded the results of 840 pupils and area B recorded the results of 900 pupils in this subject. The pie charts show the percentages obtained in the appropriate levels at KS3. How many more pupils obtained level 7 in area B compared to those gaining level 7 in area A?

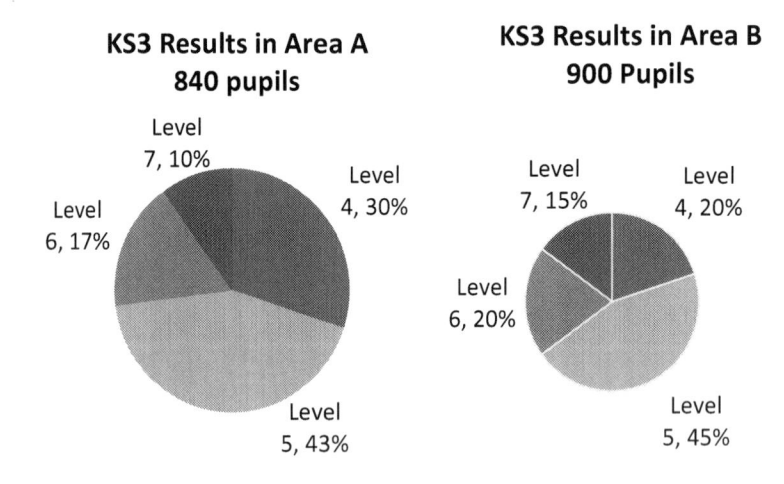

KS3 Results in Area A
840 pupils

- Level 7, 10%
- Level 6, 17%
- Level 4, 30%
- Level 5, 43%

KS3 Results in Area B
900 Pupils

- Level 7, 15%
- Level 6, 20%
- Level 4, 20%
- Level 5, 45%

Method: The percentage of pupils who get level 7 in area A is 10%. This means 10% of 840 pupils get this level. 10% of 840 = $\frac{10}{100} \times 840 = 84$ pupils.

Similarly in area B, 15% of 900 pupils get level 7.

15% of 900 = $\frac{15}{100}$ × 900 = 135 pupils. This means area B has 135 – 84 more pupils = 51 more pupils who get level 7 compared to A

Bar charts

Bar charts can be represented in columns or as horizontal bars. They can be either simple bar charts that show frequencies associated with data values or they can be multiple bar charts to allow for comparisons between data sets as shown below. The examples below illustrate some of the ways bar charts can be used to represent data.

Example 1: In a cosmetics shop the number of items that were sold for four top brands over a one month period were recorded as shown in the bar chart below.

(1) Which brand had the highest sales? **You can see from the column bar chart below that Brand D had the highest sales as 40 items of this brand were sold during one month, which is higher than any other brand**

(2) What was the proportion of sales for Brand D compared to the total? Give your answer as a fraction in its lowest terms. **The number of Brand A items sold were 20, Brand B were 35 and Brand C were 25 and as we saw earlier 40 items of Brand D were sold. This means the total number of cosmetic items sold during this one month period = 120. Since 40 items belonged to Brand D, compared to the total this is $\frac{40}{120}$ which simplifies to $\frac{1}{3}$**

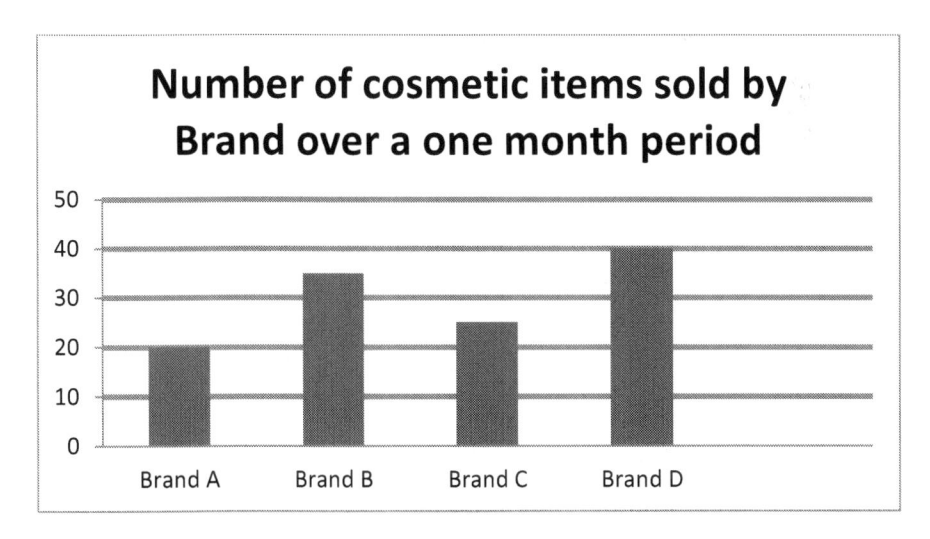

Number of cosmetic items sold by Brand over a one month period

Example 2:

The bar chart below shows the amount of time in hours John, Bob and Bill spend surfing the web at weekends. What is the mean time per boy that is spent surfing the web at the weekend?

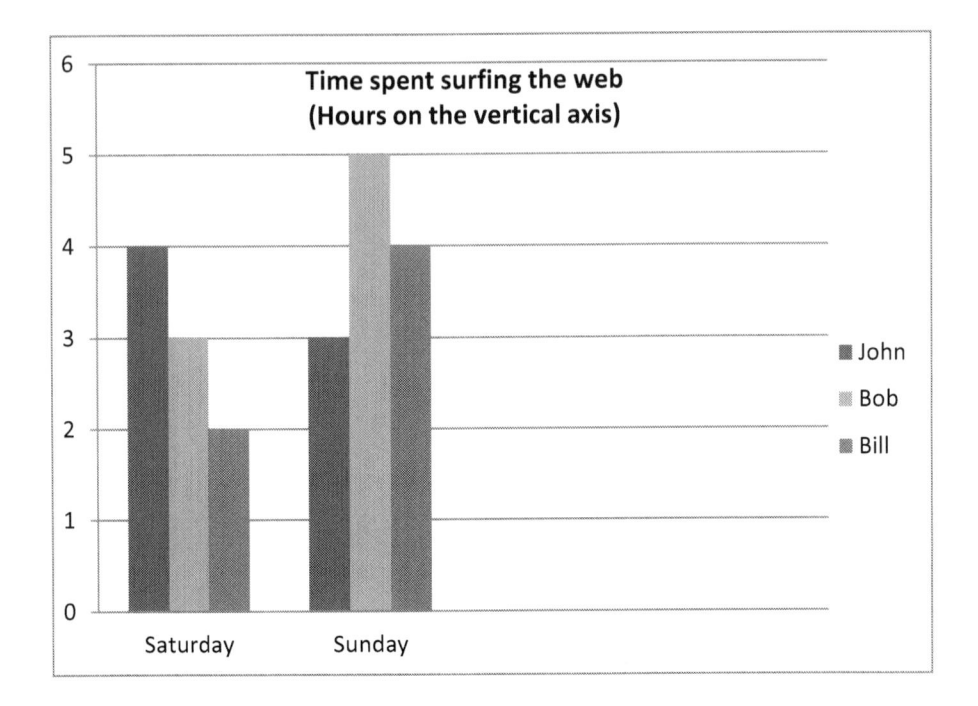

Time spent surfing the web
(Hours on the vertical axis)

Method: John spends 4 hours on Saturday and 3 hours on a Sunday: a total of 7 hours

Bob spends a total of 3 hours on Saturday and 5 hours on Sunday: a total of 8 hours

Similarly, Bill spends a total of 2 + 4 = 6 hours on a weekend

Total time spent surfing between the 3 boys on a week end is 7+ 8 + 6 =21hours

Hence the mean time spent per boy is 21 ÷ 3 =7 hours

Example 3: Horizontal Bar Chart

In an on-line company the percentage of employees in 4 key departments is shown below. (1) If there are 560 employees altogether, how many are in the On-line marketing department? (2) How many more employees are there in On-line marketing compared to Customer Service department?

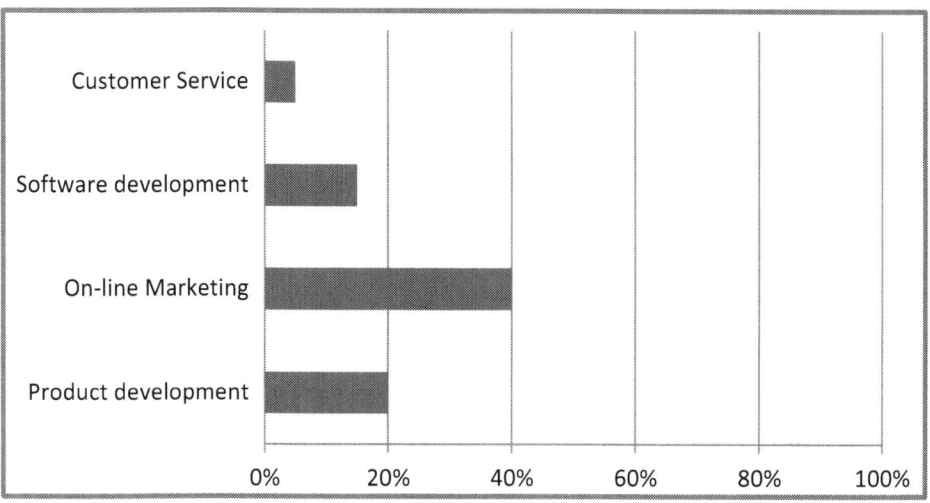

Percentage of employees in different departments in an online company

Department	Percentage
Customer Service	5%
Software development	15%
On-line Marketing	40%
Product development	20%

Method:

(1) From the bar chart you can see that 40% of the employees are in on-line marketing. Since there are 560 employees altogether, this means 40% of 560 = 224 employees
(10% of 560 = 56, hence 40% = 4×56 = 4×50 + 4×6 = 200 + 24 = 224)
(2) 5% of employees are in customer service. Since there are 560 employees altogether, 10% = 56 and 5% = 28 employees. We know from the previous question that there are 224 employees in On-line marketing. 224 − 28 = 196 employees. This means there are 196 more employees in the On-line marketing department compared to the Customers Service Department.

Example 4:

This composite bar chart below shows the percentage of pupils in a particular school who take and do not take additional lessons in music and maths respectively. What is the proportion of pupils who take extra music lessons? Give your answer as a fraction in its lowest terms.

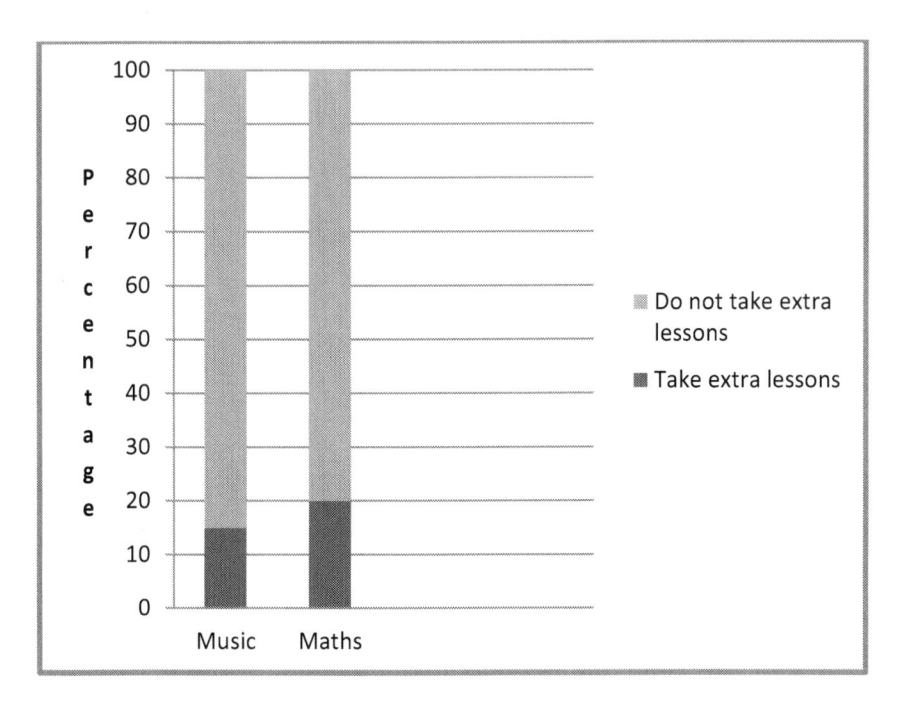

Method: The proportion of pupils who take extra music lessons is 15%. This is $\frac{15}{100}$ which simplifies to $\frac{3}{20}$. Hence $\frac{3}{20}$ of the pupils take extra lessons in music.

Example 5:

The composite bar chart below shows the number of cartons of Orange Juice, Pineapple Juice and Mango Juice sold in a local Supermarket on a given Saturday, Sunday and Monday. The vertical axis represents the number of fruit juice cartons sold.

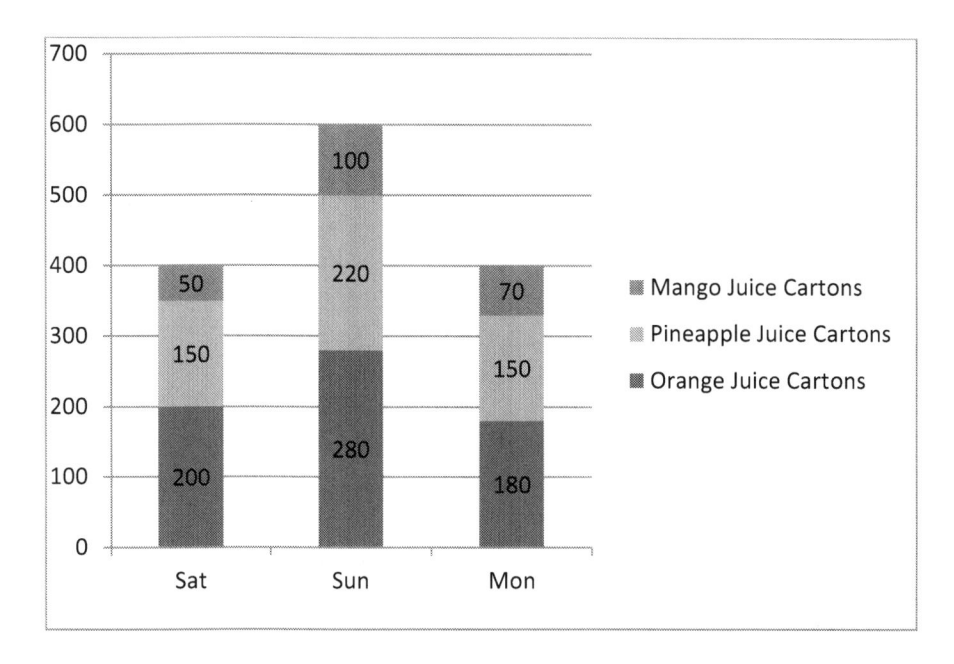

(Although a composite bar chart consists of single bars, these bars are split into two or more sections. These sections show the frequencies of the appropriate categories. Frequency in the above example is the different number of fruit cartons sold on different days.)

Example 1: On which day did this supermarket sell the highest number of mango juice cartons?

Clearly by looking at the composite graph you can see that on Sunday 100 cartons of Mango Juice were sold which is more than sold on Saturday or Monday.

Example 2: What was the proportion of pineapple juice cartons sold compared to the total of all drinks on all three days.

Method: Total Pineapple Juice cartons = 150 +220 +150 =520. Total of all three drinks sold = 400 (on Sat) + 600 (on Sun) and 400 (on Mon) = 1400 cartons of drinks.

So the proportion of pineapple cartons sold = **520÷1400 = 52÷140 =26÷70**

Or, $\frac{13}{35}$

Line graph

A line graph is a way to represent two sets of related data. **It is often used to show trends**

Example1: The data below shows the percentage of candidates who had 'A' level mathematics who were short-listed for the first interview when applying to a consultancy company. This data is shown in the table below. However, the same data can be shown as a line graph that follows.

Year	2005	2006	2007	2008	2009	2010
% of candidates with 'A' level Maths	26%	35%	45%	37%	48%	32%

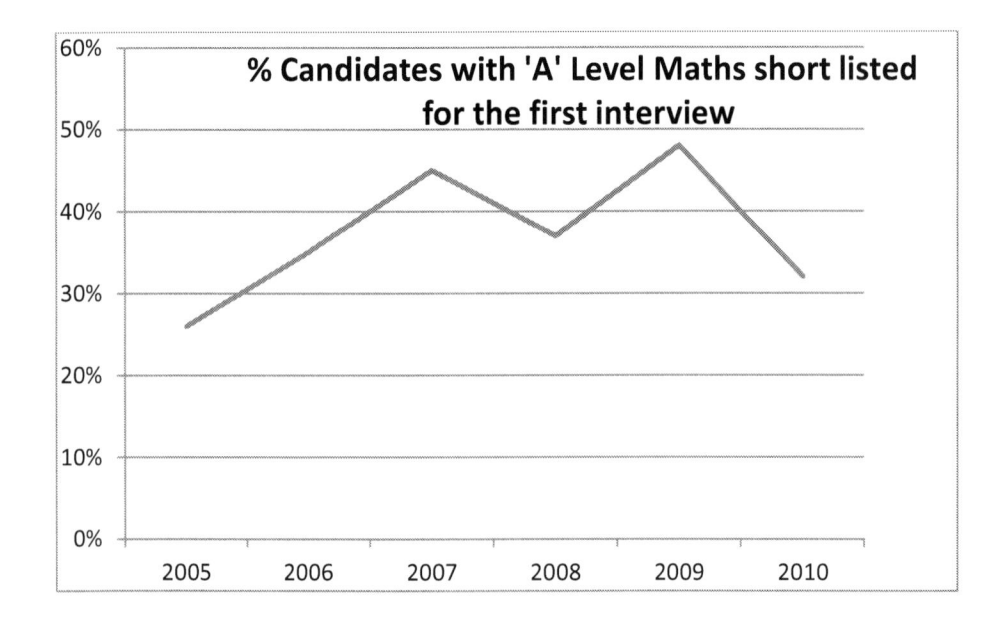

% Candidates with 'A' Level Maths short listed for the first interview

What was the change in percentage points for candidates that were short-listed between 2008 and 2010?

Method: You can see from the table as well as the graph that the success rate actually dropped from (approx.) 37% to (approx) 32%. That is decreased by 5% points.

Example 2:

The sales of Company A and Company B are plotted in a line graph from 2001 to 2006. If 850 employees worked for Company A and 800 employees worked for Company B in 2006. What was the sales per employee for Company B in 2006?

Sales of Company A and Company B from 2001 - 2006 in £ million

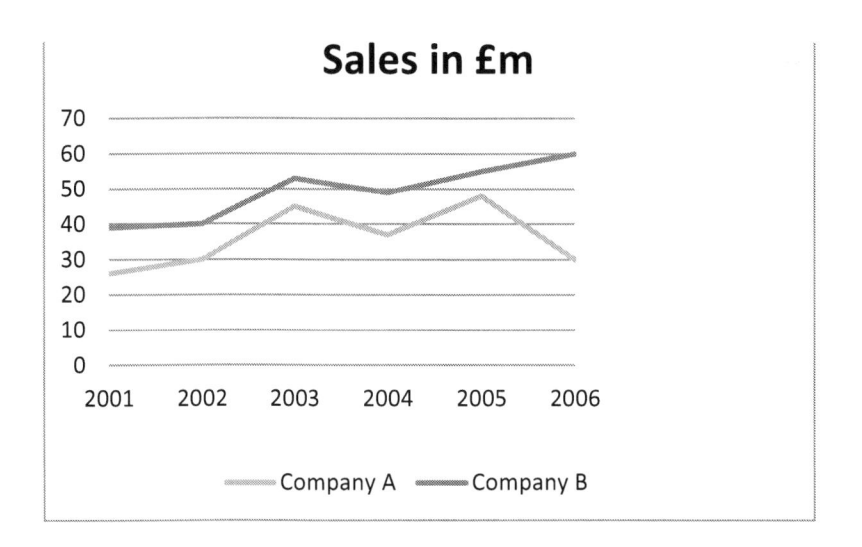

Sales in £m

```
70
60
50
40
30
20
10
 0
    2001   2002   2003   2004   2005   2006

         ——— Company A   ——— Company B
```

Method: From the line graph it can be seen that in 2006, Company B had a sales of £60 million. If 800 employees worked for this company, then clearly the sales per employee was £60,000,000 ÷ 800 = 600,000÷8 = 300,000÷4 =150,000÷2 = £75000. Hence, the sales per employee in Company B in 2006 was £75000.

Two way tables

These are used to compare data between two variables. For example, comparing the different modes of transport (one variable) used by different schools (second variable), say inner city schools and suburban schools. Example 1 demonstrates this.

Example 1:

		Method of Transport			
		Car	Bus	Walking	Other
Type of Schools	Inner City	28%	32%	24%	16%
	Suburban	62%	18%	12%	8%

From the data above you can see that 32% of children take the bus in Inner City schools compared to 18% who take the bus in suburban schools. Similarly, 62% of pupils in suburban schools arrive by car as compared to 28% in inner city schools. You can also compare other modes of transport between the two schools.

Chapter 12: Basic Algebra

The word 'algebra' comes from the Arabic al-jebr, which means 'the reuniting of broken parts'. By implication this means the equating of like to like.

In algebra we often use letters instead of numbers. There are some basic conventions and rules of algebra that you should be familiar with to progress in this subject. This chapter will be useful for you if you have forgotten your algebra.

If you see	We Mean
$x = y$	x equals y
$x > y$	x is greater than y
$x < y$	x is less than y
$x \geq y$	x is greater than or equal to y
$x \leq y$	x is less than or equal to y
$x + y$	the sum of x and y
$x - y$	subtract y from x
xy	x times y
x/y	x divided by y
$x \div y$	x divided by y
x^n	x to the power n
$x(x + y)$	x times the sum of x + y

Also note that:

$x(x+y) = x^2 + xy$

$x^2(x + x^2 + y) = x^3 + x^4 + x^2 y$

In general, a × a × a × a ....(n times) $= a^n$

You also need to know these algebraic rules for the multiplication and division of positive and negative numbers.

Multiplying positive and negative numbers.

(+) × (+) = +   (a plus number times a plus number gives us a plus number)

(+) × (−) = −   (a plus number times a minus number gives us a minus number)

(−) × (+) = −   (a minus number times a plus number gives us a minus number)

(−) × (−) = +   (a minus number times a minus number gives us a plus number)

Dividing positive and negative numbers.

(+) ÷ (+) = +   (a plus number divided by a plus number gives us a plus number)

(+) ÷ (−) = −   (a plus number divided by a minus number gives us a minus number)

(−) ÷ (+) = −   (a minus number divided by a plus number gives us a minus number)

(−) ÷ (−) = +   (a minus number divided by a minus number gives us a plus number)

Summary: <u>For both multiplication and division, like signs gives us a plus sign and unlike signs gives a minus sign</u>

Also when adding and subtracting it is worth knowing that:

When you add two minus numbers you get a bigger minus number.

Example 1: $-4 - 6 = -10$

When you add a plus number and a minus number you get the sign corresponding to the bigger number as shown below:

Example 2: $+6 - 9 = -3$, whereas, $-6 + 9 = 3$

When you subtract a minus from a plus or minus number you need to note the results as shown below:

Example 3: $6 - (-3)$ we get $6 + 3 = 9$ (since $-(-3) = +3$)

Example 4: $7 - (+3)$ we get $7 - 3 = 4$ (since $-(+3) = -3$)

In this case note that $-(-) = +$. Also, $+(-) = -$ and $-(+) = -$.

Remember the **BIDMAS** rule you were introduced to earlier which specifies the rules concerning the order in which you carry out arithmetical operations:

Simplifying algebraic expressions

Example 1: Simplify $3x + 4x + 5x$

Method: We simple add up all the x's.

Hence we get $3x + 4x + 5x = 12x$

Example 2: Simplify $3x + 4x + 3y + 5y$

Method: Add up all the like terms.

So we get $3x + 4x + 3y + 5y = 7x + 8y$

(Notice we add up all the x's and then all the y's)

Example 3: Simplify 3m +4y +2m −3y

Method: as before, we add and subtract like terms.

Now 3m+2m =5m and 4y-3y =1y or just y.

So we can write 3m +4y +2m −3y = 5m + y.

Multiplying out brackets.

Example 1: Expand 3(2x +5)

Method: we multiply 3 by each term in the bracket. So we get 3 × 2x + 3 × 5 which gives us 6x + 15.

Example 2: Expand and simplify 3(2x +5) +4(2x+7)

Method: Multiply 3 by each term in the first bracket then 4 by each term in the second bracket. The final step is to simplify by collecting up the like terms.

3(2x+5) +4(2x+7) =6x+15+8x+28 =14x + 43

Notice the last step is simply adding 6x + 8x and then 15+28.

Example 3: Work out (2x+3)(2x+4)

When we have to multiply out two brackets we have to multiply each term in the first bracket by each term in the second bracket. We then simplify the resulting expression as before. An easy way to multiply out two brackets is to use the grid method as shown below:

First put each of the terms of each bracket on the outside grid as shown

X	2x	+3
2x		
+4		

Step2: Multiply each outside term together. So that for example 2x X 2x = $4x^2$. The other results are shown inside the grid.

X	2x	+ 3
2x	$4x^2$	+ 6x
+ 4	8x	+12

After multiplying out the terms, the answer is found by adding all the terms inside the grid and simplifying the resulting expression.

So we have, $4x^2$ + 6x + 8x +12 (These are all the terms inside the grid)

Finally, $4x^2$ + 6x + 8x +12 = $4x^2$ +14x +12

Another example will help consolidate the process:

Multiply out (2x – 3)(3x +2)

Put the terms of each bracket on the outside of the grid as shown

X	2x	–3
3x	$6x^2$	– 9x
+ 2	4x	– 6

Collecting up all the terms inside the grid we have:

$6x^2$ – 9x + 4x – 6

Now simplify which gives us, $6x^2$ – 5x – 6

Algebraic Substitution

This is the process of substituting numbers for letters and working out the value of the corresponding expression.

Example 1: if a =5 and b=6 work out 2a +3b

Method: Substitute numbers for letters and we get:

2 × 5+3 × 6

(Notice 2a means 2 × a and 3b means 3 × b)

So, 2 × 5 +3 × 6 = 10+18 =28

This means that 2a+3b =28

Example 2: If m=7 and n=8 work out 5m– 3n

Substituting numbers for letters we get:

5 × 7 – 3 × 8 = 35 – 24= 11

So 5m –3n =11

Example 3: If k=6 and t=8 work out 2(4k–2t) +kt

Substituting the values of k and t we have:

2(4 X 6–2 X 8) + 6 X 8

=2 X (24-16) +48 = 2 X 8 +48 =16+48 =64

So 2(4k-2t) +kt = 64

Example 4: If t=9 and u= 6 work out $3t^2 - 5u$

Substituting appropriately we get:

$3 \times 9^2 - 5 \times 6 = 3 \times 81 - 30 = 243 - 30 = 213$

(Notice, we use the BIDMAS rule to work out the square first and then do the multiplication)

So, $3t^2 - 5u = 213$

Simple Equations

Consider the following English statements and their mathematical equivalent:

English Statements	**Algebra**
Something plus five equals ten	$x + 5 = 10$
Something times two, plus five equals eleven	$2x + 5 = 11$
Something times three, minus five equals thirteen	$3x - 5 = 13$
Something divided by two equals three	$x/2 = 3$

Now consider solving these equations using a common sense approach.

Example 1: Something plus five equals ten. What is 'something'?

Clearly we need to add five to five to get ten. So 'something' in this case equals five.

Solving this by algebra can be very similar. As we saw, we can re-write the English statement above in algebra as follows:

$x + 5 = 10$ (notice, we are representing 'something' by x)

Now, if $x + 5 = 10$ clearly x (which represents 'something') is equal to 5.

So, x=5

Example 2: 'Something' times two plus five equals eleven. Find the 'something'.

We know that 'something' times two plus five equals eleven.

So the two times 'something' must equal 6. In which case 'something' must be 3.

Now consider the algebraic equivalent.

$2x + 5 = 11$

This means $2x = 6$

Which means x=3

Now consider a more formal method.

Imagine an equation like a balance. Whatever you do to one side you must do to the other.

Example 3: Solve the equation x + 5 = 10

Subtract 5 from both sides

So, x =5

However, we can also use the method of taking inverses.

The rules are: When something is added to the x-term subtract, when something is subtracted from the x-term then add. When x, is multiplied, by a number we divide. Finally, when the x-term, is divided, by a number we multiply.

Slightly harder equations:

Example 1: Solve the equation 5x – 1= 2x +8

First add 1 to both sides, which gives:

5x = 2x +9

Now subtract 2x from both sides to give 3x = 9

Finally divide both sides by 3 to get x=3.

(Notice each step simplifies the equation further)

Example 2: Solve the equation 5(2x +1) =4(2x +1)

To solve this first multiply out the brackets which gives:

10x +5 = 8x +4

(Multiply each term outside the bracket by each term inside the bracket)

Now subtract 5 from both sides, which gives:

10x =8x –1

Now subtract 8x from both sides, which gives:

2x = –1

Finally, divide both sides by 2 to get x= –1/2 or –0.5

Example 3: Solve the inequality 2x +5>9

This simply says 2x + 5 is greater than 9. To find x still use the rules of a simple equation. That is, whatever you do to one side you must do to the other.

If 2x +5>9

Then 2x >4 (by taking away 5 from both sides)

Now, divide both sides by 2 to get x >2. Our answer for x is all values greater than 2.

Word problems (using algebra):

Example 1:

Two people collect the same amount of money each for a charity. The fund raising organisation adds £500.50 and the total amount they collect including their contribution is £1100.70. How much does each person collect?

To solve this algebraically, let the amount each person collect be x. This means $2x + £500.50 = £1100.70$ (2 times the amount each person collects plus the £500.50 the fund raising organisation contributes = £1100.70)

In the equation, $2x + 500.50 = 1100.70$, we now have to Subtract 500.50 from both sides, So we are left with $2x = 600.20$

Now divide both sides by 2(that is, take the inverse of X2)

So, x = £300.10, This means each person collects £300.10

Example 2:

John has £22 more than Brian. Altogether they have £68. How much do they each have?

Let the amount Brian has be £x

Since Brian's amount plus John's amount = £68, we can write algebraically that $x + x + 22 = 68$.

Simplifying this expression we get $2x + 22 = 68$

Subtracting 22 from both sides we get:

$2x = 46$, now divide both sides by 2. We get $x = 23$

Hence Brian has £23, and John has £45

Example 3: (Simultaneous equations where you have two unknowns in this case)

The sum of two numbers is 30. Their difference is 12. What are the two numbers?

Method: Let one of the numbers be x and the other y.

So we can deduce that (1) x + y = 30 and (2) x – y = 12.

If you add the left **and** right hand sides of the two equations then we can eliminate y. That is x + y + x –y = 30 + 12. This simplifies to 2x = 42, or x =21. Now that we have found x, we can substitute for x in the first equation. i.e. (1) to give us 21 + y = 30. By subtracting 21 from both sides we can find that y = 9. Hence the two numbers are 21 and 9.

Practice Test

Before we try the Mock Test in Numerical Reasoning let us do a practice test. This test consists of 20 questions. Allow yourself 30 minutes and try and get at least 12 questions correct - you may use paper and pencil but no calculators are allowed.

(1) Work out 27×17

(2) Find 15% of £300

(3) What is $124 \div 100$

(4) What is $327 \div 0.1$

(5) Find $2\frac{3}{4}$ of 460 miles

(6) If I travel 60km in 2.5 hours, what is my average speed?

(7) There are 21 employees in a small company. Three of them go on a special training course. What is the fraction of employees that do not go on this training course? Give your answer in its lowest terms.

(8) 2500 millilitres of liquid is divided into 20 containers. How many millilitres of liquid does each container have?

(9) A walking group walks 24 Km every week. If 8km is approximately equal to 5 miles, estimate how many miles the weekly walk consists of?

(10) 18 people are asked to collect £3.50 each for a charity. All of them succeed. What is the total amount collected?

(11) A group activity consists of 16 tasks. Each task lasts 15 minutes. How many hours will this group activity last?

(12) A meeting begins at 10:50. There is a general introduction for 6 minutes, a power-point presentation for 18 minutes and finally a question and answer session for 26 minutes. When does the meeting end? Give your answer using the 24-hour clock.

(13) A company calculated that it had given bonuses to its junior and senior staff in the ratio of 1:3. There was a total of £68000 bonus given. Assuming there were 20 senior staff, how much did each member of the senior staff get?

(14) A teacher has to see 16 parents for 12 minutes each to discuss pupil progress. In addition there is a 25 minute break. How long does the parents' session last in hours and minutes?

(15) A walking trip was organized. The map showed a scale of 1:100000. The main organizer planned out the route as follows:

Start from A and going to B total distance on the map =2.7cm

From B to C the distance on the map was 3.2 cm

Finally the distance from C to D was 8.2 cm

What was the distance in Kilometres from A to D?

(16) An assistant meteorologist wants to convert a temperature of 25 degrees Celsius into Fahrenheit

The formula for converting the temperature from Celsius to Fahrenheit is given by:

$F = \frac{9}{5} C + 32$ (where C is the temperature in degrees Celsius).

If the temperature is 25 degrees Celsius what is the equivalent temperature in Fahrenheit?

(17) The sum of two numbers is 30 and the difference between them is 8. What are the two numbers?

(18) In one school 140 pupils took GCSE maths exams. Both the percentage of pupils as well as the GCSE Grades obtained in maths is shown in the pie chart below.

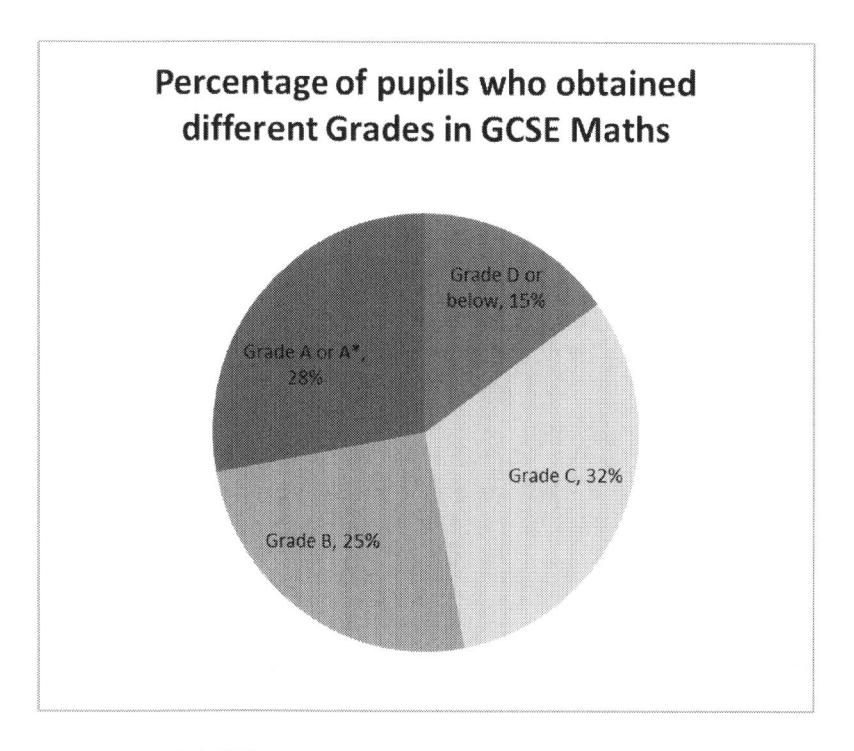

Percentage of pupils who obtained different Grades in GCSE Maths

- Grade D or below, 15%
- Grade A or A*, 28%
- Grade C, 32%
- Grade B, 25%

(a) What was the number of pupils who got Grade B?

(b) What was the percentage of pupils who got Grade C or above?

(19) The area of a rectangle is 162 m^2. The length of the rectangle is two times the width. What is the length and width of the rectangle?

(20) The cost of a coat after a 20% discount is £85. What was its original price?

Answers to Practice Test

1. 27 ×17 = 459
   Method 27×17 = 27×10 + 27×5 +27×2 =270 +135+54 = 459
2. 15% of £300 = £45
   Method: 10% =£30 & 5% = £15. Hence total = £45
3. 124 ÷ 100 = 1.24
4. 327 ÷ 0.1 =3270 (remember when dividing by 0.1, you are effectively dividing by one tenth)
5. $2\frac{3}{4}$ of 460 = 1265 miles
   Method: double 460 + half of 460 + a quarter of 460 = 920 +230 +115 = 1265 miles
6. Average Speed = 24km/hour
   Method: Speed = Distance÷Time = 60÷2.5 = 24
7. The number of employees that do not go on a training course is $\frac{6}{7}$
   Method: Number of employees that do not go on a training course is 18. Hence fraction of employees that do not go = $\frac{18}{21}$ which simplifies to $\frac{6}{7}$ (Divide the top and bottom numbers of $\frac{18}{21}$ by 3)
8. Each container has 125ml of liquid
   Method: 2500 ÷ 20 =125
9. The weekly walk consists of 15miles. Method: Since 8km = 5miles then 24 km =24×$\frac{5}{8}$ = 120÷ 8 = 60 ÷ 4 = 15
10. Total amount collected = £63

    Method: 18×3 + 0.5×18 =54 + 9 =£63

11. The group activity lasts for 4hours
    Method: 16× 15 =16×10 + 16×5 = 160 + 80 =240 minutes = 4hrs

12. The meeting ends at 11:40
    Method: 6+ 18 + 26 = 50 minutes. Add 50 mins to 10:50 to get 11:40

13. Each senior member gets £2550
    Method: Total parts in ratio = 4, therefore each part = 68000/4 = £17000. Senior staff get 3× as much = £51000. Since there are 20 senior staff each member of the senior staff gets £2550

14. The parents' session lasts 3 hours and 37 minutes
    Method: 16 × 12 +25 (min break) = 192 +25 = 217 minutes
    Since 180 minutes = 3 hours, we are left with 37 minutes. Hence total time taken = 3 hours 37 minutes

15. 14.1 km

    Method: Total distance on the map = 2.7 + 3.2 + 8.2 = 14.1 cm. Using a scale 1:100000. This means 14.1cm =14.1×100000cm = 1410000cm = 14100 metres (divide 1410000 by 100 to give the answer in metres). Finally, 14100 ÷1000 = 14.1 km

16. 77° Fahrenheit

    Method: In the formula $F= \frac{9}{5}C +32$ substitute C = 25 so we get $F= \frac{9}{5} \times 25 +32 = 45 + 32 = 77$ degrees fahrenheit

17. The two numbers are 19 & 11

    Method: Let the two numbers be x and y. So x + y = 30 and

    x − y = 8. Add the two equations to get 2x = 38. Hence x = 19 and y =11 since x+y =30

(18) (a) 35 pupils

Method: 25% of 140 = $\frac{1}{4}$ of 140 = 35

(b) 85%

Method: From the pie chart it can be seen that 32% got a grade C, 25% got a grade B and 28% got grade A or A*. Hence the total percentage who got a grade C or above is 32% + 25% + 28% = 85%

(19) Width = 9m and Length = 18m

Method: Let the width = w and the length = 2w. We know that the area of a rectangle is length × width = 2w×w = $2w^2$. The area of the rectangle is given as $162m^2$. Hence, $2w^2$ = 162. Dividing both sides by 2, we get w^2 = 81. Hence w = $\sqrt{81}$ = 9. So the width is 9m and the length is 18m.

(20) The original price was £106.25

Method: Let the original price be £x. This means x − 20% of x = 85 or x − 0.2x = 85, which simplifies to 0.8x =85. Now divide both sides by 0.8. We get x = 85÷0.8 = 106.25. Hence the original price is £106.25 (Note: to work this out without a calculator 85÷0.8 is the same as 850÷8 = 425÷4 = 400÷4 + 25÷4 = 100 +6$\frac{1}{4}$ = £106.25)

Numerical Reasoning Mock Test

Mostly Data interpretation with Multiple Choice questions

When you take the numerical reasoning test you might have 36 questions to answer in 15 minutes and no calculators will be allowed. You will, however, be allowed to use paper and pencil. In the test below you will find each question has four parts to answer. So although there are 9 questions you will find there are 36 questions in total. Some of the questions below are probably slightly harder than the ones you are likely to get. Don't worry if it takes you 25 - 30 minutes to complete this test. Try and get at least 22 questions correct.

No calculators allowed

Question 1

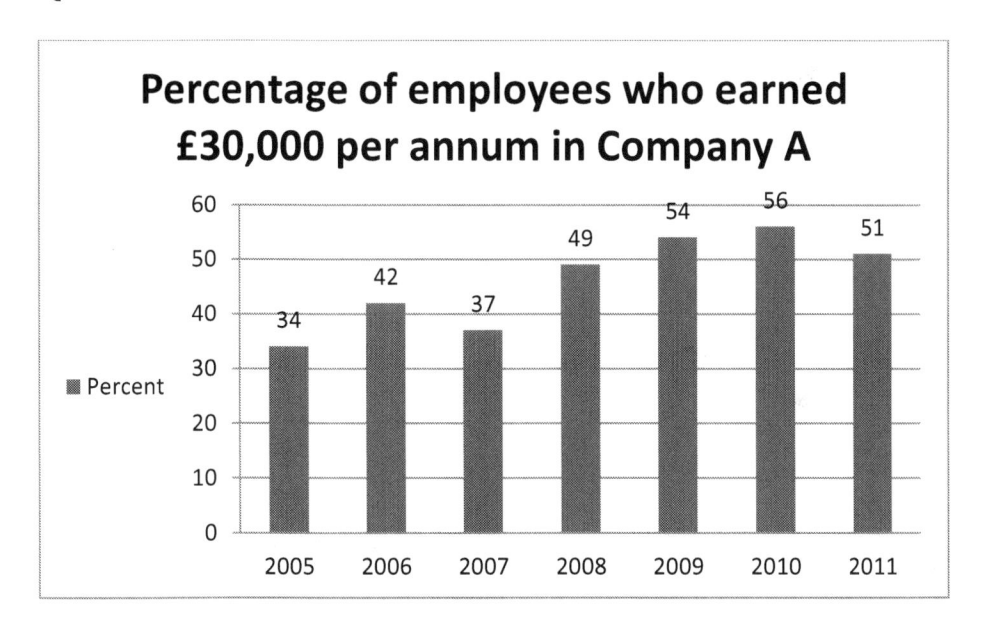

Percentage of employees who earned £30,000 per annum in Company A

Year	2005	2006	2007	2008	2009	2010	2011
Percent	34	42	37	49	54	56	51

(1) Which year had the highest percentage of employees earning £30,0000
   (a) 2008   (b) 2011   (c) 2009   (d) 2010   (e) 2006
(2) The mean percentage who earned £30,000 from 2008 to 2011 was:
   (b) 20%   (b) 21%   (c) 37%   (d) 52.5%   (e) 24.5%

(3) What was the percentage increase in employees that earned £30,000 from 2005 to 2011?
  (c) 26%   (b) 28%   (c) 17%   (d) 40%   (e) 50%

(4) The decrease in percentage <u>points</u> between 2010 and 2011 of employees earning £30,000 was
  (a) 7%   (b) 8%   (c) 51%   (d) 5%   (e) Can't tell

Question 2

A teacher wanted to compare the progress of 8 pupils across two tests and see who had increased by at least 10 percentage points. The first test was out of 40 and the second test was out of 50.

Pupils	Test1 (marks out of 40)	Test 2 (marks out of 50)
A	22	32
B	25	32
C	17	27
D	25	35
E	19	26
F	12	20
G	25	34
H	30	47

(1) What was the percentage score obtained by Pupil H in Test 1
  (a) 65%   (b) 70%   (c) 75%   (d) 60%   (e) 30%
(2) What was the percentage score of pupil F in Test 2
  (a) 20%   (b) 40%   (c) 50%   (d) 45%   (e) 60%
(3) Which two pupils scored the same marks in Test 1
  (a) A & B   (b) A & C   (c) B & G   (d) A & H   (e) Can't tell
(4) The average percentage marks gained by pupil F in both tests was
  (a) 33%   (b) 35%   (c) 42%   (d) 31%   (e) Can't tell

Question 3

Report: The number of emergency admissions at 4 Hospitals on three days in the UK

Hospital	Friday	Saturday	Sunday
Hospital A	200	210	90
Hospital B	180	160	100
Hospital C	250	150	60
Hospital D	150	120	20

(1) Which hospital had the most admissions for all three days combined?

(a) Hospital B (b) Hospital A (c) Hospital D (d) Hospital C (e) Can't tell

(2) What is the percentage of admissions in Hospital A on a Sunday compared to all Hospitals on the same day?

(a) 31.33% (b) 29.33% (c) 33.33% (d) 40% (e) Can't tell

(3) The total admissions in all 4 hospitals on Sunday was:

(a) 275 (b) 260 (c) 270 (d) 280 (e) 370

(4) The difference in admissions between Hospital B and C on Friday was:

(a) 80 (b) 70 (c) 85 (d) 90 (e) Can't tell

Question 4

Report: **E-Reader Sales in millions for March 2011**

Country	Kindle	Ipad	Nook
USA	2	1.5	0.02
UK	0.5	0.3	0.01
Germany	0.4	0.35	0.02
France	0.35	0.45	0.03

(1) How many Nook e-readers in thousands were sold in Europe during this month?
   (a) 8000   (b) 80,000   (c) 81,000   (d) 810,000   (e) 60000

(2) Which country had the least Kindle & Ipad sales combined?

   (a) USA   (b) UK   (c) Germany   (d) France   (e) Can't tell

(3) In which country besides the USA were ipad sales the most popular?

   (a) France   (b) USA   (c) UK   (d) Germany   (e) Can't tell

(4) How many more Kindles were sold compared to Ipads in the USA in thousands?

   (a) 50,0000   (b) 55,0000   (c) 500,000   (d)) 0.5 million   (e) 510,000

Question 5

Annual sales report for 4 medium sized companies in 2010

Company	Annual Sales	Number of employees
A	£4 million	50
B	£6 million	100
C	£2.4 million	60
D	£8 million	160

(1) Which Company had the highest annual sales?

(a) Company A (b) Company B (c) Company C (d) Company D

(2) What was the sales per employee in Company C?

(a) £120,000   (b) £40,000   (c) £400,000   (d) £4,000   (e) £110,000

(3) Which Company had the highest sales per employee?

(a) Company A (b) Company B (c) Company C (d) Company D

(4) What was the proportion of sales in Company A compared to Company D?

(a) $\frac{1}{3}$ (b) $\frac{4}{10}$ (c) $\frac{1}{2}$ (d) $\frac{1}{5}$ (e) Can't tell

Question 6

The graph below shows the percentage of pupils achieving Grade C in Maths from 2006 to 2011.

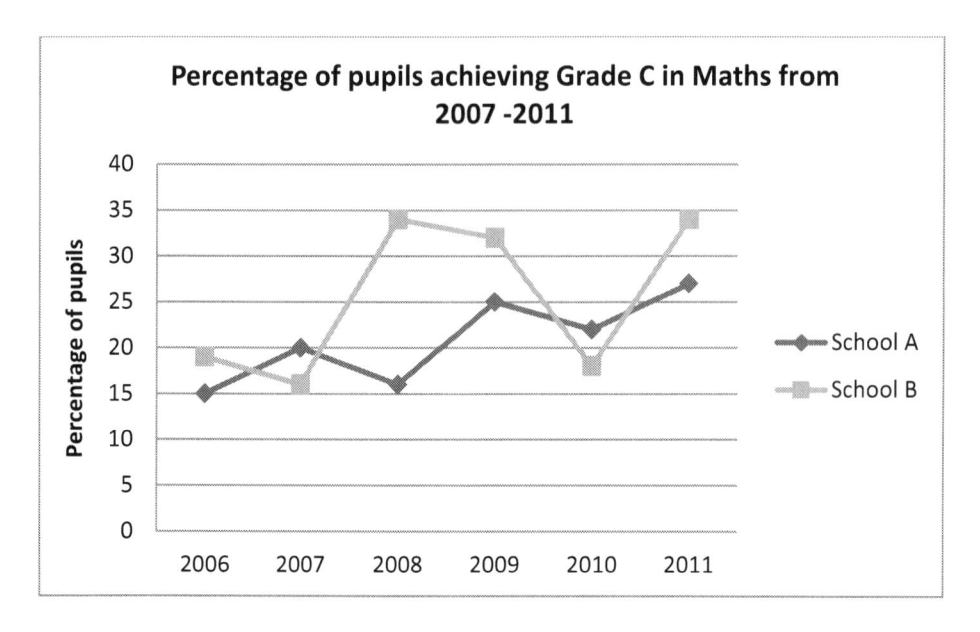

Percentage of pupils achieving Grade C in Maths from 2007 -2011

(1) By how many percentage points **approximately** did School B outperform School A in maths in 2011?
 (a) 17% (b) 7% (c) 10% (d) 15% (e) 12%

(2) What was the percentage point increase in achieving Grade C Maths in School A from 2006 to 2009?
 (a) 15% (b) 10% (c) 20% (d) 5% (e) 25%

(3) What was the average percentage of pupils who obtained a grade C in maths in both schools A & B in 2007?
 (a) 17.5% (b) 30% (c) 40% (d) 45% (e) Can't tell

(4) What was the percentage of pupils who did not achieve a grade C in Maths in school A in 2009?

(a) 70% (b) 25% (c) 35% (d) 75% (e) Can't tell

Question 7

The Deputy Head created the following table showing the number of pupils in each year group who had music lessons.

Year Group	Number of pupils	Number of pupils who have music lessons
7	92	10
8	101	18
9	105	14
10	96	13
11	102	11

(1) What is the percentage of pupils in all the year groups combined that have music lessons? Give your answer rounded to a whole number.

(a) 21% (b) 13% (c) 19% (d) 20% (e) 22%

(2) The total number of pupils in year 7, 8 & 9 were:

(a) 290 (b) 398 (c) 298 (d) 280 (e) 258

(3) The proportion of pupils who have music lesson in year 11 is:

(a) $\frac{11}{101}$ (b)) $\frac{13}{96}$ (c)) $\frac{11}{102}$ (d)) $\frac{1}{10}$ (e) Can't tell

(4) The number of pupils who did <u>not</u> have music lessons in year 10 was:

(a) 82 (b) 73 (c) 75 (d) 83 (e) Can't tell

Question 8

The table below shows the total sales by a fashion retailer in London, Paris and New York

Total Sales	2008	2009	2010	2011
London shops (In Millions of £)	11.0	9.8	8.0	10.0
Paris shops (In Millions of Euros)	7.7	7.8	6.9	8.2
New York shops (In Millions of $)	15.0	14.3	14.6	18.0

(1) Assuming that in 2013 on average the exchange rates was £1 = 1.25 Euros and £1 = 1.6 US $. What were the total sales in 2013 in London in US dollars.
   (a) $16.1M   (b) $1.6M   (c) $16M   (d) $6.1M   (e) Can't tell

(2) What was the increase in Sales in Paris from 2008 to 2009, giving your answer in thousands of Euros?

   (a) 70000 euros (b) 100,000 euros (c) 110,000 euros (d) 10,000 euros (e) 1M euros

(3) What was the percentage increase in sales in New York from 2008 to 2011?
   (a) 25%   (b) 30%   (c) 20%   (d) 40%   (e) Can't tell

(4) In 2012 what was the sales in London when converted to Euros, give your answer in millions?
   (a) 9m euros (b) 10m euros (c) 8.25m euros (d) 11m euros (e) Can't tell

Question 9

A distribution centre serves stores within a radius of 40 miles. The table below shows the distance in miles of each store from the distribution centre.

Distance from the distribution centre	Number of stores
10 miles or less	7
11 to 20 miles	16
21 to 30 miles	12
31 to 40 miles	15

(1) How many stores are there 25 miles or more from the distribution centre?
   (a) 7   (b) 12   (c) 28   (d) 11   (e) Can't tell

(2) What is the distance from the distribution centre where most stores are located?
   (a) 10 miles or less (b) 11 to 20 miles (c) 21 to 30 miles (d) 31 to 40 miles (e) can't tell

(3) How many stores does the distribution centre serve?
   (a) 46   (b) 56   (c) 45   (d) 50   (e) Can't tell

(4) What percentage of stores are 11 miles or more from the distribution centre?
   (a) 76% (b) 85%   (c) 86%   (d) 90%   (e) 75%

Answers to Mock Test

Question 1

(1) Answer (d) 2010

Method: The highest bar on the percentage (vertical) axis is 2010 which corresponds to (d)

(2) Answer (d) 52.5%

Method: The mean % of those that earned £30,000 from 2008 to 2011 = (49 + 54 + 56 + 51)/4 = 210÷4 =52.5%

(3) Answer: (e) 50%

Method: Increase in percentage points from 2005 to 2011 = 17%

This increase of 17% was from 34%. To find the percentage increase we calculate $\frac{17}{34} \times 100 = \frac{1}{2} \times 100 = 50\%$ (Notice you can simplify $\frac{17}{34}$ to be equal to $\frac{1}{2}$ (cancel top and bottom by 17)

(4) Answer (d) 5%

Method: Difference between 2010 and 2011 = 56% - 51% = 5% points

Question 2

(1) Answer: (c) 75%

Method: Convert pupil H's score into a percentage. Since pupil H got 30 out of 40 marks. This corresponds to $\frac{30}{40}$ which simplifies to $\frac{3}{4} = 75\%$

(Note: $\frac{3}{4} \times 100 = \frac{300}{4} = \frac{150}{2} = 75\%$)

(2) Answer: (b) 40%

Method: Pupil F got 20 out of 50 in Test 2. This corresponds to $\frac{20}{50}$ which simplifies to $\frac{2}{5}$. To convert this fraction into a percentage we multiply it by 100. Hence $\frac{2}{5} \times 100 = \frac{200}{5} = 40\%$

(3) Answer: (c) pupils B & G

Method: Look down the first column (Test 1 marks) and you will see that pupils B & G have the same marks

(4) Answer: (b) 35%

Method: In Test 1 pupil F gained $\frac{12}{40} = \frac{6}{20} = \frac{3}{10}$ marks or 30%

Similarly, in Test 2 pupil F gained $\frac{20}{50} = \frac{2}{5}$ or $\frac{2}{5} \times 100 = \frac{200}{5} = 40\%$

So the average for both tests is: $\frac{30+40}{2} = \frac{70}{2} = 35\%$

Question 3

(1) Answer: (b) Hospital A

Method: The total admissions for the three days at the 4 hospitals were as follows: A =500, B = 440, C = 460, D = 290. Hence hospital A had the most admissions

(2) Answer: (c) 33.33%

Method: Total admission on Sunday for the four hospitals = 90 + 100 +60 +20 =270. So percentage for Hospital A is $\frac{90}{270} \times 100 = \frac{1}{3} \times 100 = 33.33\%$

(3) Answer: (c) 270

Method: Simply add all the admissions for all hospitals on Sunday: 90 + 100 + 60 + 20 = 190 + 80 = 270

(4) Answer: (b) 70

Method: The difference between admissions at Hospital B and Hospital C on Friday was 250 − 180 = 70

Question 4

(1) Answer: (e) 60,000

Method: The number of Nook E-readers sold in Europe (UK, Germany & France) for March 2011 = (0.01 + 0.02 + 0.03) million

= 0.06 million = 0.06 × 1000000 = 60,000

(2) Answer: (c) Germany

Method: Combined Kindle & Ipad sales by country is USA = 3.5M, UK = 0.8m, Germany = 0.75M, France = 0.8m. Hence, the least sales were in Germany.

(3) Answer: (a) France

Method: Look down the column of Ipad sale, ignoring USA. From the remaining countries clearly France is the most popular

(4) Answer: 500,000

Method: USA kindle sales = 2million, USA ipad sales = 1.5 million

Difference in sales is 2m − 1.5m = 0.5million = 500,000

Question 5

(1) Answer (d) Company D

Method: look down the column of annual sales. Clearly company D has the highest sales

(2) Answer (b) £40,000

Method: The Annual sales in company C was £2.4M and there were 60 employees. Hence the sales per employee in this company was £2.4M ÷60 = 2,400,000÷60 = 240,000÷6 = £40,000

(3) Answer (a) Company A

Method: The sales per employee can be worked out by dividing the annual sales of each company by the number of employees.

Company A = £4m ÷50 =£80,000; Company B =£6m ÷100=£60,000; Company C= £2.4m÷60 =£40,000 and Company D=£8m÷160= £50,000. Hence Company A has the highest sales per employee

(4) Answer: (c) $\frac{1}{2}$

Method: Sales in Company A = £4m, Sales in Company D = £8m hence the proportion of sales of the two respective companies are $\frac{4}{8} = \frac{1}{2}$

Question 6

(1) Answer (b) 7% (approximately)

Method: From the line graph in 2011, school A achieved approx. 27% success in achieving Grade C in Maths.

Similarly, school B achieved 34%. Hence the difference was 7%

(2) Answer (b) 10%

Method: From the line graph the percentage of pupils achieving the GCSE grade C success changed from 15% in 2006 to 25% in 2009. Hence this amounted to an increase in 10 percentage points.

(3) (a) 17.5%

Method: The percentage of pupils who got a grade C in Maths in Schools A & B in 2007 were 15% and 20% respectively. Hence the average percentage success at this grade was $\frac{15+20}{2} = \frac{35}{2} = 17.5\%$

(4) (d) 75%

Method: The percentage of pupils who got a grade C in Maths in school A in 2009 is 25%. Hence the percentage of pupils who did not get a grade C is 100 − 25 =75%

Question 7

(1) Answer: (b) 13%

Method: Total number of pupils = 496. Total number of pupils who have music lessons = 66. Hence percentage of pupils who have music lesson =$\frac{66}{496}$× 100 = approx. 13%

(2) Answer: (c) 298

Method: Simply add the number of pupils in Year 7, 8 & 9. So we get 92 + 101 + 105 = 193 + 105 =298

(3) Answer: (c) $\frac{11}{102}$

Method: The number of pupils who have music lessons in year 11 is 11. The total in this year group is 102. Hence the proportion who have music lessons is 11 out of 102 = $\frac{11}{102}$

(4) Answer: (d) 83

Method: The number of pupils who had music lessons in year 10 = 13. The total in this year group is 96. Hence the number of pupils that did not have music lessons in this year group is 96 − 13 = 83

Question 8

(1) Answer (e) Can't tell

Method: No data is given for 2013

(2) Answer (d) 100,000 euros

Method: increase in sales in Paris from 2008 to 2009 = 7.8 -7.7 = 0.1M million euros. This is the same as 0.1 ×1000,000 = 100,000 euros

(3) Answer: (c) 20%

Method: The increase in sales in New York from 2008 to 2011 was 18m − 15m =3m. Hence the percentage increase in sales was: $\frac{3}{15}$ ×100 = $\frac{300}{15}$ = 20%

(4) Answer: (e) Can't tell

Method: No data is given for 2012

Question 9

(1) Answer: (e) Can't tell

Method: Although we can calculate the total number of stores from 21 miles onwards, we do not have specific information from 25 miles onwards

(2) Answer: (b) 11 to 20 miles

Method: You can see from the stores column that the mode (the most frequently occurring number is 16 and this corresponds to (b) 11 to 20 miles.

(3) Answer: (d) 50

Method: The total number of stores within a radius of 40 miles can simply be found by adding all the stores in this range. 7 + 16 + 12 + 15 = 23 + 27 = 50

(4) Answer: (c) 86%

Method: The number of stores that are more than 11 miles way = 16 + 12 + 15 = 28 + 15 = 43. There are a total of 50 stores from the distribution centre. This corresponds to $\frac{43}{50} \times 100 = 86\%$